P9-CKK-850

PRESENTED TO

By

DATE

OCCASION

GOD'S WORD
FOR EVERY
CIRCUMSTANCE

Revised Edition

GOD'S WORD FOR EVERY CIRCUMSTANCE

Revised Edition

Compiled by
CASEY & WENDY TREAT

ISBN 0-931697-36-0

Published by Christian Faith Center
P.O. Box 98800
Seattle, WA 98198

TABLE OF CONTENTS

PREFACE

The Word of God is alive and powerful. Hebrews 4:12 says: "For the word of God is living and powerful, and sharper than any two-edged sword, piercing even to the division of soul and spirit, and of joints and marrow, and is a discerner of the thoughts and intents of the heart."

The life and power of the Word cannot be received from any other source. Only God's message to men and women can bring freedom, strength, and life. Only the Word of God contains the power to save, heal, deliver, and meet every need. People have looked for these results in every possible place: religion, alcohol and drugs, sex and romance, and money and power, but they never find life's answers and their needs are never met through these things.

God has exalted His Word even above His Name. Heaven and earth will pass away, but the Word of God will not. When you build your life on God's Word, you are building on the most solid foundation in the universe. Jesus says that the fool hears the Word but does not do it, so his house (life) is built on sand. The wise man hears the Word and does it, and his house (life) is built on a rock. The storms of life come to both, but only one will stand. He is the one who built his life on the rock; the one who lives the Word of God.

Paul says in II Timothy 3:16-17, "All Scripture is given by inspiration of God, and is profitable for doctrine, for reproof, for correction, for instruction in righteousness, that the man of God may be complete, thoroughly equipped for every good work."

As you use the principles in these pages as tools to overcome the mountains in your life and to answer the questions you face, I believe you will experience God's power working in you. I believe you'll find the "profit" God has given you in the Word, and I trust you will be fully equipped for every good work.

Sincerely,

Casey Treat

PRAYING THE LORD'S PRAYER

Jesus gave six prayer topics in Matthew 6:9-13:

I. "Our Father in heaven, hallowed be Your name."
    A. We start this first "prayer lap" by recognizing God as our Father by the blood of Jesus.
        Colossians 1:12-14
    B. His name is holy, set apart, to be praised and adored.
        John 14:12; Philippians 2:9-11
        1. We have power in the name of Jesus.
        2. All prayer results are because of His name.
    C. We praise the Father for His names and benefits revealed by the Word:
        1. Jehovah-Tsidkenu, Lord our righteousness.
        2. Jehovah-M'Kaddesh, Lord who sanctifies.
        3. Jehovah-Shalom, Lord our peace.
        4. Jehovah-Shammah, Lord is there.
        5. Jehovah-Rapha, Lord who heals.
        6. Jehovah-Jireh, Lord sees and provides.
        7. Jehovah-Nissi, Lord our banner.
        8. Jehovah-Ra'ah, Lord our shepherd.

D. These eight names reveal five benefits for believers:
   1. Sin - forgiveness and deliverance from sin.
      II Corinthians 5:21
   2. Spirit - fullness of the Holy Spirit.
      I Corinthians 3:16
   3. Soundness - health and healing.
      I Peter 2:24
   4. Success - freedom from the curse of the law.
      Philippians 4:13
   5. Security - freedom from fear of death and Hell.
      Hebrews 2:14-15
E. As we worship and praise the name of the Lord, the Holy Spirit can work these benefits in our lives.
F. We have authority in the name of Jesus.
   Mark 16:17-18
   John 16:33
   Philippians 2:9-11

II. "Your kingdom come. Your will be done on earth as it is in heaven."
A. We start this prayer lap by confessing that God's kingdom and His will are the top priorities of our lives.
   Matthew 6:33; Romans 14:17
   1. We must confess our surrender to God's will and mean it.
   2. God's kingdom is His presence and authority in our lives.

Luke 17:20-21

B. Pray for yourself to deal wisely with the day ahead and succeed.
   1. You must be plugged in to God's will for today.
   2. You are not begging but seeking and believing for God's kingdom power.
C. Pray for your family to fulfill God's will for the day.
   1. Pray for your mate.
   2. Pray for your children.
   3. Pray for relatives.
D. Pray for your church and leadership:
   1. Pastors
   2. Church leaders
   3. Congregation
   4. Harvest
      Isaiah 43:4-6
E. Pray for the U.S. and other nations.
   1. Mission teams
   2. World leaders
      Psalm 122:6; I Timothy 2:1-2
F. Through prayer we are calling for heaven on earth.
   1. God's will is for us to succeed.
   2. His will is good for every area of life.

III. "Give us this day our daily bread."
   A. On this prayer lap we are praying for our daily needs in all areas of life.
   B. God desires to bless all areas of our lives with His abundance.
      John 10:10; Philippians 4:19; III John 2

1. Wisdom and knowledge
2. Favor with people
3. Health and strength
4. Finances

C. We are not begging but believing for God's supply.
Matthew 21:22; Mark 11:24

D. To receive God's abundance we must live in God's will.
Isaiah 1:19-20; Malachi 3:8-11;
I Thessalonians 4:11-12;
II Thessalonians 3:10-15; James 1:25

E. We must believe it is God's will for us to prosper.
Deuteronomy 8:18; Deuteronomy 28:1-4;
Psalm 35:27; Mark 10:29-30;
James 1:5-8

F. We must be specific in our requests.
Mark 10:51; John 15:7

G. Don't give up, stand in faith, and be tenacious.
Luke 18:1-8

IV. "And forgive us our debts, as we forgive our debtors."

A. On this prayer lap we examine and cleanse our personal lives and our relationships.

B. We start by examining ourselves for sin or impurity.
I Corinthians 11:28-30
1. Debt is fault, something owed, sin.
2. Don't deceive yourself, be real.

C. God has called us to be holy in thought and action.
   Ephesians 4:22-24; I Peter 1:15-16
   1. Repent of wrong motives.
   2. Change wrong actions.
D. We will not be free from sin until we confess it and repent of it.
   James 5:16; I John 1:9
E. Part of being clean and holy is forgiving your debtors.
   Matthew 6:14-15; Mark 11:24-26 (Amp.)
F. You will be cut off from the Father's blessings and in torment as long as you hold unforgiveness.
   Matthew 18:21-35; Luke 6:38;
   I Peter 3:7-11
   1. This hinders the answer to our prayers.
   2. We reap the same bitterness we sow.
G. We hold others in bondage to their sin and open the door for the spirit of sin to come on us through unforgiveness.
   John 20:23
H. By following this point of Jesus' prayer guide we will stay at peace with ourselves and all those around us.
   Matthew 5:9

V. "And do not lead us into temptation, but deliver us from the evil one."
   A. On this prayer lap we stand against the attacks of the devil and seek God's deliverance.

B. We must first recognize Satan is the tempter.
Luke 4:1-2; I Thessalonians 3:5; James 1:12-17

C. We are praying, "Father lead us away from Satan's temptation and save us from his evil attacks."

D. Temptation is an opportunity for growth and to glorify God in victory.
Daniel 3:17-25; James 1:2-4
   1. Through temptations, tests, and trials we can grow strong.
   2. As your spiritual muscles are tested, you'll get in better shape.
   Luke 4:1-14

E. It is never God's will for you to be defeated or broken through trials.
I Corinthians 10:13; I Peter 5:6-9

F. As we follow the Holy Spirit He will lead us away from evil and on to victory.
Psalm 23; Romans 8:14,16

G. If we are in any evil, God can and will deliver us.
Psalm 91:3-11

VI. "For Yours is the kingdom and the power and the glory forever. Amen."

A. On this prayer lap we praise God for answered prayer, giving Him all the glory, and we pray in tongues for things we don't know about.

B. Before we "see" the results of our prayer, we praise and thank God by faith,

knowing it shall come to pass.
Mark 11:24; Philippians 4:6-7

C. We praise God and give Him all the glory
    for what is done.
    Hebrews 13:15; Psalm 103:1-5
D. There are seven different Hebrew words
    for praise:
    1. Todah - extend hands in thanks-
        giving.
    2. Yadah - worship with extended
        hands, throw out the hands enjoying
        God.
    3. Hallal - vigorously excited to laud,
        boast, rave, celebrate.
    4. Zamar - praise with song, pluck
        strings.
    5. Barak - to bless; to declare God is the
        origin of success, prosperity, fertility;
        to be still.
    6. Tehillah - singing in the spirit,
        singing hallals.
    7. Shabach - commend, address in a
        loud tone, shout.
        Psalm 150
E. Praise in every situation releases the
    power of God to bring answered prayer.
    Jonah 2:7-10; Acts 16:25-34
F. Praying in tongues allows the Holy Spirit
    to pray through us when we don't know
    what to pray.
    Romans 8:26-28
    1. We are speaking in the Spirit to the
        Father.

7

I Corinthians 14:2

2. It is for all people.
    John 1:33; Acts 1:4-5;
    Acts 2:4,38-39; Mark 16:17

G. Benefits to praying in tongues:
1. Build up the inner man.
    I Corinthians 14:4
2. Receive revelation knowledge.
    I Corinthians 14:2
3. Enables you to hear the voice of your spirit.
    I Corinthians 14:14
4. Intercede for things you don't know about.
    Romans 8:26
5. Pray the perfect will of God.
    Romans 8:27
6. Builds you up on your faith.
    Jude 20
7. Brings rest and refreshing.
    Isaiah 28:11-12
8. Helps us keep our tongue in line with the Word.
    James 3:6,8-10
9. Gives thanks and magnifies God.
    I Corinthians 14:16-17
10. Tongues are a sign to unbelievers.
    I Corinthians 14:22

AMBASSADORS

An ambassador is one who goes with authority and represents his own country in various countries. He knows full well the authority his country has given him, and he exercises that authority.

We are to go and do the work of the ministry. We are to represent our kingdom and our God with all power and authority, knowing the calling we have on our lives. As God's ambassador, you carry the authority to speak God's Word. Let it come out of your mouth boldly, with power and authority, to meet the needs of the people.

<u>Won By One</u>, Wendy Treat

Proverbs 13:17
A wicked messenger falls into trouble, but a faithful ambassador brings health.

Malachi 2:7
For the lips of a priest should keep knowledge, and people should seek the law from his mouth; for he is the messenger of the LORD of hosts.

John 14:12-14
Most assuredly, I say to you, he who believes in Me, the works that I do he will do also; and greater works than these he will do, because I go to My Father. And whatever you ask in My name, that I will do, that the Father may be glorified in the Son. If you ask anything in My name, I will do it.

John 17:18
As You sent Me into the world, I also have sent them into the world.

II Corinthians 5:20
Now then, we are ambassadors for Christ, as though God were pleading through us: we implore you on Christ's behalf, be reconciled to God.

Ephesians 6:20
For which I am an ambassador in chains; that in it I may speak boldly, as I ought to speak.

Renewal Thought:
God has given you the ministry of reconciliation, and He has said that He is your sufficiency. He has made you an able minister. He made you an ambassador.

ANGER

When your mind is negative, you bring forth disagreement, fighting, and bitterness. You bring forth anger and depression, and other negative things of life.

People use the old saying, "I got up on the wrong side of the bed," to excuse the bad things coming out of the negative treasure in their hearts. But the side of the bed you get up on has nothing to do with the fruit in your life. Others may say, "Well, I'm just in a bad mood." No, it is not a "mood"; it is a way of thinking.

<u>Being Spiritually Minded</u>, Casey Treat

Psalm 37:8
Cease from anger, and forsake wrath; do not fret—it only causes harm.

Proverbs 15:1
A soft answer turns away wrath, but a harsh word stirs up anger.

Proverbs 16:32
He who is slow to anger is better than the mighty, and he who rules his spirit than he who takes a city.

Matthew 5:38-42
You have heard that it was said, "An eye for an eye and a tooth for a tooth." But I tell you not to resist an evil person. But whoever slaps you on your right cheek, turn the other to him also. If anyone wants

to sue you and take away your tunic, let him have your cloak also. And whoever compels you to go one mile, go with him two. Give to him who asks you, and from him who wants to borrow from you do not turn away.

Ephesians 2:1-3
And you He made alive, who were dead in trespasses and sins, in which you once walked according to the course of this world, according to the prince of the power of the air, the spirit who now works in the sons of disobedience, among whom also we all once conducted ourselves in the lusts of our flesh, fulfilling the desires of the flesh and of the mind, and were by nature children of wrath, just as the others.

Ephesians 4:26,31-32
Be angry, and do not sin: do not let the sun go down on your wrath. . . Let all bitterness, wrath, anger, clamor, and evil speaking be put away from you, with all malice. And be kind to one another, tenderhearted, forgiving one another, just as God in Christ forgave you.

Ephesians 6:4
And you, fathers, do not provoke your children to wrath, but bring them up in the training and admonition of the Lord.

Colossians 3:21
Fathers, do not provoke your children, lest they become discouraged.

James 1:19
So then, my beloved brethren, let every man be swift
to hear, slow to speak, slow to wrath.

RENEWAL THOUGHT

*Life and death, blessing or cursing are set before
you to choose. Which one do you want? You control what you choose. But then, what you choose
controls you. So choose carefully!*

AUTHORITY

If we realize there is a problem in our home, we begin to say, "Father, I pray in the name of Jesus for the comfort of the Spirit, for the peace of the Spirit, for your blessing upon our home." But we don't just talk to the Father. We begin to talk to the enemy that we're warring against. This is important to realize because too often we don't go into battle - we just talk to God about the battle. If we just talk to God about the mountain, we never get into the battle. The Lord has given you His Name. He gave you the authority. He gave you the weaponry. Don't talk to God about the problem. Get into spiritual warfare and say, "You demons who have come into my house to bring strife, I bind you in the name of Jesus! I cast you out and command you to go!"

Fighting For Excellence In Leadership, Casey Treat

Matthew 7:29
For He taught them as one having authority, and not as the scribes.

Matthew 8:5-10,13
Now when Jesus had entered Capernaum, a centurion came to Him, pleading with Him, saying, "Lord, my servant is lying at home paralyzed, dreadfully tormented." And Jesus said to him, "I will come and heal him." The centurion answered and said, "Lord, I am not worthy that You should come under my roof. But only speak a word, and my servant will be healed. For I also am a man under

authority, having soldiers under me. And I say to this one, 'Go,' and he goes; and to another, 'Come,' and he comes; and to my servant, 'Do this,' and he does it." When Jesus heard it, He marveled, and said to those who followed, "Assuredly, I say to you, I have not found such great faith, not even in Israel!" Then Jesus said to the centurion, "Go your way; and as you have believed, so let it be done for you." And his servant was healed that same hour.

Matthew 28:18-20
And Jesus came and spoke to them, saying, "All authority has been given to Me in heaven and on earth. Go therefore and make disciples of all the nations, baptizing them in the name of the Father and of the Son and of the Holy Spirit, teaching them to observe all things that I have commanded you; and lo, I am with you always, even to the end of the age." Amen.

Mark 16:17-18
And these signs will follow those who believe: In My name they will cast out demons; they will speak with new tongues; they will take up serpents; and if they drink anything deadly, it will by no means hurt them; they will lay hands on the sick, and they will recover.

Luke 4:36
Then they were all amazed and spoke among themselves, saying, "What a word this is! For with authority and power He commands the unclean spirits, and they come out."

15

Luke 10:19
Behold, I give you the authority to trample on serpents and scorpions, and over all the power of the
enemy, and nothing shall by any means hurt you.

Ephesians 1:16-23
Do not cease to give thanks for you, making mention of you in my prayers: that the God of our Lord
Jesus Christ, the Father of glory, may give to you
the spirit of wisdom and revelation in the knowledge of Him, the eyes of your understanding being
enlightened; that you may know what is the hope
of His calling, what are the riches of the glory of
His inheritance in the saints, and what is the exceeding greatness of His power toward us who believe, according to the working of His mighty power
which He worked in Christ when He raised Him
from the dead and seated Him at His right hand in
the heavenly places, far above all principality and
power and might and dominion, and every name
that is named, not only in this age but also in that
which is to come. And He put all things under His
feet, and gave Him to be head over all things to the
church, which is His body, the fullness of Him who
fills all in all.

Hebrews 13:17
Obey those who rule over you, and be submissive,
for they watch out for your souls, as those who must
give account. Let them do so with joy and not with
grief, for that would be unprofitable for you.

RENEWAL THOUGHT

Prayer and the Name of Jesus give us the authority to bind the work of the devil and loose the work of God.

Baptism Of
The Holy Spirit

The baptism with the Holy Spirit is a necessary part of the successful Christian life. Jesus did not suggest to His disciples that they be baptized with the Holy Spirit, He commanded them to wait in Jerusalem and go nowhere until they had been endued (filled) with power from on high. If we are disciples of Jesus, that commandment is still for us today. Jesus wants you to be filled with the Holy Spirit and receive the power therein to live victoriously in every aspect of life.

Living the New Life, Casey Treat

Luke 11:13
If you then, being evil, know how to give good gifts to your children, how much more will your heavenly Father give the Holy Spirit to those who ask Him!

Acts 1:5
For John truly baptized with water, but you shall be baptized with the Holy Spirit not many days from now.

Acts 2:4
And they were all filled with the Holy Spirit and began to speak with other tongues, as the Spirit gave them utterance.

Acts 2:38
Then Peter said to them, "Repent, and let every one

of you be baptized in the name of Jesus Christ for the remission of sins; and you shall receive the gift of the Holy Spirit.

Acts 8:17
Then they laid hands on them, and they received the Holy Spirit.

Acts 10:44
While Peter was still speaking these words, the Holy Spirit fell upon all those who heard the word. And those of the circumcision who believed were astonished, as many as came with Peter, because the gift of the Holy Spirit had been poured out on the Gentiles also. For they heard them speak with tongues and magnify God.

I Corinthians 14:2,4,14,15
For he who speaks in a tongue does not speak to men but to God, for no one understands him; however, in the spirit he speaks mysteries. He who speaks in a tongue edifies himself, but he who prophesies edifies the church. For if I pray in a tongue, my spirit prays, but my understanding is unfruitful. What is the conclusion then? I will pray with the spirit, and I will also pray with the understanding. I will sing with the spirit, and I will also sing with the understanding.

RENEWAL THOUGHT
When you're born again and filled with the Holy Spirit, God is in you and working with you. You have His presence and His power.

BEING IN CHRIST

God dwells in you. God walks in you. When you walk, God walks. When you show up, God shows up. When you show up, a winner shows up. You won't lose. The Bible says God dwells in me. Does God lose? Then how can I lose? The only way I can lose is when I get out of line with God and start doing my own thing, and then it's hard telling what's going to happen.

The Bible says whosoever shall confess that Jesus is the Son of God will have God dwelling in them. It didn't say whoever cleans up their life, and changes everything, and becomes 100% pure and holy; God dwells in them.

Casey Treat

Acts 17:28
For in Him we live and move and have our being, as also some of your own poets have said, "For we are also His offspring."

Romans 8:1-2
There is therefore now no condemnation to those who are in Christ Jesus, who do not walk according to the flesh, but according to the Spirit. For the law of the Spirit of life in Christ Jesus has made me free from the law of sin and death.

I Corinthians 1:30
But of Him you are in Christ Jesus, who became

20

for us wisdom from God— and righteousness and sanctification and redemption.

II Corinthians 5:17
Therefore, if anyone is in Christ, he is a new creation; old things have passed away; behold, all things have become new.

II Corinthians 5:21
For He made Him who knew no sin to be sin for us, that we might become the righteousness of God in Him.

Galatians 3:26
For you are all sons of God through faith in Christ Jesus.

Philippians 4:13
I can do all things through Christ who strengthens me.

I John 5:14-15
Now this is the confidence that we have in Him, that if we ask anything according to His will, He hears us. And if we know that He hears us, whatever we ask, we know that we have the petitions that we have asked of Him.

RENEWAL THOUGHT
We are winners only because God walks in us, and God dwells in us.

BEING LED BY THE SPIRIT

God has a way of letting us know what is right, what is wrong, and what His will is. Call it a feeling, a knowing, an intuition, or a green light on the inside, we all have a witness in our spirit when something is in question. You get a witness about certain opportunities and whether or not you should "go" or "not go."

This is not usually an audible voice, just a witness in our heart. It is a spiritual directive about what we should do or not do. Even people who do not know God have some ability to discern. But for the Christian, the Holy Spirit is inside to tell us what to do.

   Fulfilling Your God-Given Destiny, Casey Treat

Psalm 32:8
I will instruct you and teach you in the way you should go; I will guide you with My eye.

Psalm 48:14
For this is God, our God forever and ever; he will be our guide even to death.

Psalm 73:24
You will guide me with Your counsel, and afterward receive me to glory.

Psalm 119:11
Your word I have hidden in my heart, that I might not sin against You!

Isaiah 42:16
I will bring the blind by a way they did not know; I will lead them in paths they have not known. I will make darkness light before them, and crooked places straight. These things I will do for them, and not forsake them.

John 16:13
However, when He, the Spirit of truth, has come, He will guide you into all truth; for He will not speak on His own authority, but whatever He hears He will speak; and He will tell you things to come.

Romans 8:14,16
For as many as are led by the Spirit of God, these are sons of God. The Spirit Himself bears witness with our spirit that we are children of God.

I John 2:20,27
But you have an anointing from the Holy One, and you know all things. But the anointing which you have received from Him abides in you, and you do not need that anyone teach you; but as the same anointing teaches you concerning all things, and is true, and is not a lie, and just as it has taught you, you will abide in Him.

I John 5:10
He who believes in the Son of God has the witness in himself; he who does not believe God has made Him a liar, because he has not believed the testimony that God has given of His Son.

RENEWAL THOUGHT

God wants to direct your life by the Spirit within you. Let Him do it.

BODY - TEMPLE OF THE HOLY GHOST

Together, soul and spirit make up a human being - a spiritual person - who lives in a natural body. But it takes all three parts to function properly: spirit, soul and body.

God created us to function with the spirit as owner, the soul as manager, and the body as servant. If the owner and manager (administrator) are not in agreement, then the servant usually will do as he pleases. To be a working Christian, the spirit, soul, and body must all function in harmony.

True beauty is found in the hidden person of the heart, in a meek and quiet spirit. The hidden man of the heart, the spirit, is the real you. You are a spirit, created in God's likeness and in His image. You are a spirit who works through a soul. The spirit is the hidden man of the heart. When you realize who you are and begin to control your soul and body, then you can be in control of your life. And when you control the vision of your heart, you control the future.

<u>Reaching Your Destiny</u>, Casey Treat

Proverbs 23:21
For the drunkard and the glutton will come to poverty, and drowsiness will clothe a man with rags.

Ecclesiastes 10:17
Blessed are you, O land, when your king is the son of nobles, and your princes feast at the proper

time— for strength and not for drunkenness!

I Corinthians 3:16-17
Do you not know that you are the temple of God and that the Spirit of God dwells in you? If anyone defiles the temple of God, God will destroy him. For the temple of God is holy, which temple you are.

I Corinthians 6:15-20
Do you not know that your bodies are members of Christ? Shall I then take the members of Christ and make them members of a harlot? Certainly not! Or do you not know that he who is joined to a harlot is one body with her? For "the two," He says, "shall become one flesh." But he who is joined to the Lord is one spirit with Him. Flee sexual immorality. Every sin that a man does is outside the body, but he who commits sexual immorality sins against his own body. Or do you not know that your body is the temple of the Holy Spirit who is in you, whom you have from God, and you are not your own? For you were bought at a price; therefore glorify God in your body and in your spirit, which are God's.

I Corinthians 9:24-27
Do you not know that those who run in a race all run, but one receives the prize? Run in such a way that you may obtain it. And everyone who competes for the prize is temperate in all things. Now they do it to obtain a perishable crown, but we for

an imperishable crown. Therefore I run thus: not with uncertainty. Thus I fight: not as one who beats the air. But I discipline my body and bring it into subjection, lest, when I have preached to others, I myself should become disqualified.

RENEWAL THOUGHT

When a God-breathed spirit unites with a physical body, a living soul comes into being.

BOLDNESS

The Word says, "You are an able minister." As an able minister, you can boldly, and without any hesitation, minister to a person and get them born again and filled with the Holy Ghost.

God chose you, He empowered and enabled you to share His love with this world. Be the bold witness you were created to be.

<u>Won by One</u>, Wendy Treat

Proverbs 28:1
The wicked flee when no one pursues, but the righteous are bold as a lion.

Acts 4:13,29,31
Now when they saw the boldness of Peter and John, and perceived that they were uneducated and untrained men, they marveled. And they realized that they had been with Jesus. Now, Lord, look on their threats, and grant to Your servants that with all boldness they may speak Your word. And when they had prayed, the place where they were assembled together was shaken; and they were all filled with the Holy Spirit, and they spoke the word of God with boldness.

Ephesians 3:12
In whom we have boldness and access with confidence through faith in Him.

Ephesians 6:19
And for me, that utterance may be given to me, that

I may open my mouth boldly to make known the mystery of the gospel.

I Thessalonians 2:2
But even after we had suffered before and were spitefully treated at Philippi, as you know, we were bold in our God to speak to you the gospel of God in much conflict.

Hebrews 4:16
Let us therefore come boldly to the throne of grace, that we may obtain mercy and find grace to help in time of need.

Hebrews 10:19
Therefore, brethren, having boldness to enter the Holiest by the blood of Jesus.

Hebrews 13:6
So we may boldly say: "The Lord is my helper; I will not fear. What can man do to me?"

I John 4:17
Love has been perfected among us in this: that we may have boldness in the day of judgment; because as He is, so are we in this world.

RENEWAL THOUGHT
Step out on the strength of God's Word, and He'll see to it that His Word does not return to Him void.

BUSINESS

The purpose of work is not just for financial income, or as some would say, "to make a living." It also involves the fulfilling of our God-given gifts and talents - the use of our abilities, creativity and imagination. Without a place to put our spirit, soul and body to work, we would be depressed, discouraged and unfulfilled. Even if it were possible for the whole nation to live on welfare, it would never be right nor the will of God because God commands us to work with our hands and our minds for His sake and ours.

<u>God's Provision</u>, Casey Treat

Deuteronomy 28:1-3,5,8
Now it shall come to pass, if you diligently obey the voice of the LORD your God, to observe carefully all His commandments which I command you today, that the LORD your God will set you high above all nations of the earth. And all these blessings shall come upon you and overtake you, because you obey the voice of the LORD your God: Blessed shall you be in the city, and blessed shall you be in the country. Blessed shall be your basket and your kneading bowl. The LORD will command the blessing on you in your storehouses and in all to which you set your hand, and He will bless you in the land which the LORD your God is giving you.

Joshua 1:8

This Book of the Law shall not depart from your mouth, but you shall meditate in it day and night, that you may observe to do according to all that is written in it. For then you will make your way prosperous, and then you will have good success.

Psalm 1:1-3

Blessed is the man who walks not in the counsel of the ungodly, nor stands in the path of sinners, nor sits in the seat of the scornful; but his delight is in the law of the LORD, and in His law he meditates day and night. He shall be like a tree planted by the rivers of water, that brings forth its fruit in its season, whose leaf also shall not wither; and whatever he does shall prosper.

Psalm 112:5-8

A good man deals graciously and lends; he will guide his affairs with discretion. Surely he will never be shaken; the righteous will be in everlasting remembrance. He will not be afraid of evil tidings; his heart is steadfast, trusting in the LORD. His heart is established; he will not be afraid, until he sees his desire upon his enemies.

Proverbs 3:13-15

Happy is the man who finds wisdom, and the man who gains understanding; for her proceeds are better than the profits of silver, and her gain than fine gold. She is more precious than rubies, and all the things you may desire cannot compare with her.

Proverbs 4:7-8
Wisdom is the principal thing; therefore get wisdom. And in all your getting, get understanding. Exalt her, and she will promote you; she will bring you honor, when you embrace her.

III John 2-3
Beloved, I pray that you may prosper in all things and be in health, just as your soul prospers. For I rejoiced greatly when brethren came and testified of the truth that is in you, just as you walk in the truth.

RENEWAL THOUGHT
God's design for your life includes a place where you can use the gifts and talents that are in you. He wants you to enjoy prosperity through your labors.

CHILDREN

Ⅰ regularly tell my children that I love them, but I also tell them that I like them, and I enjoy being with them. I tell them that their Mom and Dad are blessed to have them as their children. I also tell them that they are blessed to have us as parents. I say, "God blessed you to put you in our home." And the same is true of your child. God blessed your child, by putting them in your home.
<u>Woman! Get In Your Place</u>, Wendy Treat

Genesis 33:5
And he lifted his eyes and saw the women and children, and said, "Who are these with you?" And he said, "The children whom God has graciously given your servant."

Genesis 48:9
And Joseph said to his father, "They are my sons, whom God has given me in this place." And he said, "Please bring them to me, and I will bless them."

Psalm 113:9
He grants the barren woman a home, like a joyful mother of children. Praise the LORD!

Psalm 127:3-5
Behold, children are a heritage from the LORD, the fruit of the womb is a reward. Like arrows in the hand of a warrior, so are the children of one's youth. Happy is the man who has his quiver full of them;

they shall not be ashamed, but shall speak with their enemies in the gate.

Proverbs 13:24
He who spares his rod hates his son, but he who loves him disciplines him promptly.

Proverbs 17:6
Children's children are the crown of old men, and the glory of children is their father.

Proverbs 19:18
Chasten your son while there is hope, and do not set your heart on his destruction.

Proverbs 22:6
Train up a child in the way he should go, and when he is old he will not depart from it.

Proverbs 22:15
Foolishness is bound up in the heart of a child; the rod of correction will drive it far from him.

Proverbs 23:13-14
Do not withhold correction from a child, for if you beat him with a rod, he will not die. You shall beat him with a rod, and deliver his soul from hell.

Proverbs 29:15
The rod and rebuke give wisdom, but a child left to himself brings shame to his mother.

Isaiah 8:18
Here am I and the children whom the LORD has given me! We are for signs and wonders in Israel from the LORD of hosts, who dwells in Mount Zion.

Matthew 19:13-15
Then little children were brought to Him that He might put His hands on them and pray, but the disciples rebuked them. But Jesus said, "Let the little children come to Me, and do not forbid them; for of such is the kingdom of heaven." And He laid His hands on them and departed from there.

Ephesians 6:1-4
Children, obey your parents in the Lord, for this is right. "Honor your father and mother," which is the first commandment with promise: "that it may be well with you and you may live long on the earth." And you, fathers, do not provoke your children to wrath, but bring them up in the training and admonition of the Lord.

RENEWAL THOUGHT

When we raise our children in the Word, they will love us and recognize the love we have for them.

CHURCH

God has already decided the church will succeed in its mission. The gates of hell will not prevail against us, and every nation will hear the Good News of the Gospel before Jesus comes again. Our ministries will prosper and grow if we walk with God and follow His plan.

<u>Building Leaders That Build a Church</u>, Casey Treat

Deuteronomy 14:2
For you are a holy people to the LORD your God, and the LORD has chosen you to be a people for Himself, a special treasure above all the peoples who are on the face of the earth.

Matthew 16:16-19
Simon Peter answered and said, "You are the Christ, the Son of the living God." Jesus answered and said to him, "Blessed are you, Simon Bar-Jonah, for flesh and blood has not revealed this to you, but My Father who is in heaven. And I also say to you that you are Peter, and on this rock I will build My church, and the gates of Hades shall not prevail against it. And I will give you the keys of the kingdom of heaven, and whatever you bind on earth will be bound in heaven, and whatever you loose on earth will be loosed in heaven."

Matthew 18:20
For where two or three are gathered together in My name, I am there in the midst of them.

Ephesians 1:22
And He put all things under His feet, and gave Him to be head over all things to the church.

Ephesians 2:19
Now, therefore, you are no longer strangers and foreigners, but fellow citizens with the saints and members of the household of God.

Ephesians 5:30
For we are members of His body, of His flesh and of His bones.

Colossians 1:18
And He is the head of the body, the church, who is the beginning, the firstborn from the dead, that in all things He may have the preeminence.

Hebrews 10:24,25
And let us consider one another in order to stir up love and good works, not forsaking the assembling of ourselves together, as is the manner of some, but exhorting one another, and so much the more as you see the Day approaching.

RENEWAL THOUGHT

The church is a manifestation of what's in the leader. With the right ingredients in you, your church will grow and glorify God.

COMFORT

The church is not going to grow and the world is not going to come to the church as long as we are talking about how ungodly, how sinful, how un-righteous, how low-down, and how good-for-nothing they are. When we begin to talk about how God loves them, how God wants to answer their prayers, how God wants to heal them, how God wants to show compassion to them, how God wants to bless them, and how God has freely given them all things, they'll start running in.

The world wants to know about the love of God. They want to hear that God is full of compassion and that His loving-kindness will heal them, save them, deliver them, and meet all of their needs. The love of God has moved out to heal everyone.

Casey Treat

Psalm 23
The LORD is my shepherd; I shall not want. He makes me to lie down in green pastures; he leads me beside the still waters. He restores my soul; he leads me in the paths of righteousness for His name's sake. Yea, though I walk through the valley of the shadow of death, I will fear no evil; for You are with me; your rod and Your staff, they comfort me. You prepare a table before me in the presence of my enemies; you anoint my head with oil; my cup runs over. Surely goodness and mercy shall follow me all the days of my life; and I will dwell in the house of the LORD forever.

Matthew 9:22
But Jesus turned around, and when He saw her He said, "Be of good cheer, daughter; your faith has made you well." And the woman was made well from that hour.

Luke 7:13
When the Lord saw her, He had compassion on her and said to her, "Do not weep."

John 14:1
Let not your heart be troubled; you believe in God, believe also in Me.

John 14:16-18
And I will pray the Father, and He will give you another Helper, that He may abide with you forever—the Spirit of truth, whom the world cannot receive, because it neither sees Him nor knows Him; but you know Him, for He dwells with you and will be in you. I will not leave you orphans; I will come to you.

John 16:33
These things I have spoken to you, that in Me you may have peace. In the world you will have tribulation; but be of good cheer, I have overcome the world.

II Corinthians 1:3
Blessed be the God and Father of our Lord Jesus Christ, the Father of mercies and God of all comfort.

I Thessalonians 5:11,14

Therefore comfort each other and edify one another, just as you also are doing. Now we exhort you, brethren, warn those who are unruly, comfort the fainthearted, uphold the weak, be patient with all.

RENEWAL THOUGHT

When Jesus sees us struggling, His compassion comes out to meet our needs.

CONDEMNATION

We must remember that we have already been judged and punished for past sins. God judged us guilty for our sins, whatever they were, small or great. God punished us with crucifixion for those things - we have already been judged and punished. So stop punishing yourself today! You were crucified with Christ and you were buried with Christ through baptism into His death. The sins of your past have been dealt with as far as God is concerned. Now you are raised with Christ to live in newness of life. God isn't worrying about your past sins and neither should you.

The devil would like to keep you thinking about your sins and shortcomings. He knows that how you think is how you will live. If Satan can keep you focused on those things, he can keep you bound up in them.

If the enemy can keep preachers condemning people and telling them they are no good - if he can keep them focused on all the bad news in the world - if he can fill their minds with negativity - he knows they will not rise up to be influential Christians.
<u>Seeing Yourself Through God's Eyes</u>, Casey Treat

John 3:17-19
For God did not send His Son into the world to condemn the world, but that the world through Him might be saved. He who believes in Him is not condemned; but he who does not believe is condemned already, because he has not believed in the

name of the only begotten Son of God. And this is the condemnation, that the light has come into the world, and men loved darkness rather than light, because their deeds were evil.

John 5:24
Most assuredly, I say to you, he who hears My word and believes in Him who sent Me has everlasting life, and shall not come into judgment, but has passed from death into life.

Romans 8:1-2
There is therefore now no condemnation to those who are in Christ Jesus, who do not walk according to the flesh, but according to the Spirit. For the law of the Spirit of life in Christ Jesus has made me free from the law of sin and death.

Romans 8:34-39
Who is he who condemns? It is Christ who died, and furthermore is also risen, who is even at the right hand of God, who also makes intercession for us. Who shall separate us from the love of Christ? Shall tribulation, or distress, or persecution, or famine, or nakedness, or peril, or sword? As it is written: "For Your sake we are killed all day long; we are accounted as sheep for the slaughter." Yet in all these things we are more than conquerors through Him who loved us. For I am persuaded that neither death nor life, nor angels nor principalities nor powers, nor things present nor things to come, nor height nor depth, nor any other created thing, shall be able to separate us from the love of God which is in

Christ Jesus our Lord.

James 5:12
But above all, my brethren, do not swear, either by heaven or by earth or with any other oath. But let your "Yes," be "Yes," and your "No," "No," lest you fall into judgment.

Renewal Thought
Don't let the guilt and thoughts of past failures keep you from living your new life. You cannot rationalize or change the past, but you can leave it behind.

CONFESSION

Confessing ownership is different than talking about your vision. Confessing it means it is now yours. It is no longer, "I am thinking about starting a business." Now it is, "I am starting a business. I am a business owner. I am doing this." Now you own the vision. Now you have to do something or keep quiet.

Reaching Your Destiny, Casey Treat

Psalm 45:1
My heart is overflowing with a good theme; I recite my composition concerning the King; my tongue is the pen of a ready writer.

Proverbs 4:24
Put away from you a deceitful mouth, and put perverse lips far from you.

Proverbs 6:2
You are snared by the words of your mouth; you are taken by the words of your mouth.

Proverbs 12:13
The wicked is ensnared by the transgression of his lips, but the righteous will come through trouble.

Proverbs 13:2
A man shall eat well by the fruit of his mouth, but the soul of the unfaithful feeds on violence.

Proverbs 18:21
Death and life are in the power of the tongue, and those who love it will eat its fruit.

Proverbs 31:26
She opens her mouth with wisdom, and on her tongue is the law of kindness.

Matthew 10:32
Therefore whoever confesses Me before men, him I will also confess before My Father who is in heaven.

Mark 11:23
For assuredly, I say to you, whoever says to this mountain, "Be removed and be cast into the sea," and does not doubt in his heart, but believes that those things he says will come to pass, he will have whatever he says.

Romans 10:9-10
That if you confess with your mouth the Lord Jesus and believe in your heart that God has raised Him from the dead, you will be saved. For with the heart one believes unto righteousness, and with the mouth confession is made unto salvation.

Hebrews 3:1
Therefore, holy brethren, partakers of the heavenly calling, consider the Apostle and High Priest of our confession, Christ Jesus.

Hebrews 4:14
Seeing then that we have a great High Priest who has passed through the heavens, Jesus the Son of God, let us hold fast our confession.

Hebrews 10:23
Let us hold fast the confession of our hope without wavering, for He who promised is faithful.

RENEWAL THOUGHT

According to the confession of your mouth, so shall it be.

CONFIDENCE

Confidence seems to be built in a back-and-forth sway between blowing it and success, and from success to not quite hitting the mark. You go through life with times of success and times of failure, all the while growing. In the "down swings," you usually think, "That was the worst I have ever done." Is that true? Challenge yourself. If you are going for God and seeking Him, then you most certainly could not be at the lowest point. Living in Jesus and seeking His ways always brings growth. So, even though you may feel you are at your lowest point, you have reached way beyond the point when you did not have Jesus.

<u>The Fulfilled Woman</u>, Wendy Treat

Proverbs 3:26
For the LORD will be your confidence, and will keep your foot from being caught.

Proverbs 14:26
In the fear of the LORD there is strong confidence, and His children will have a place of refuge.

Isaiah 30:15
For thus says the Lord GOD, the Holy One of Israel: "In returning and rest you shall be saved; in quietness and confidence shall be your strength."

Acts 28:31
Preaching the kingdom of God and teaching the

47

things which concern the Lord Jesus Christ with all confidence, no one forbidding him.

II Corinthians 5:18-19
Now all things are of God, who has reconciled us to Himself through Jesus Christ, and has given us the ministry of reconciliation, that is, that God was in Christ reconciling the world to Himself, not imputing their trespasses to them, and has committed to us the word of reconciliation.

Galatians 6:4
But let each one examine his own work, and then he will have rejoicing in himself alone, and not in another.

Ephesians 3:12
In whom we have boldness and access with confidence through faith in Him.

Hebrews 10:35-39
Therefore do not cast away your confidence, which has great reward. For you have need of endurance, so that after you have done the will of God, you may receive the promise: "For yet a little while, and He who is coming will come and will not tarry. Now the just shall live by faith; but if anyone draws back, my soul has no pleasure in him." But we are not of those who draw back to perdition, but of those who believe to the saving of the soul.

I John 5:14-15
Now this is the confidence that we have in Him,

that if we ask anything according to His will, He hears us. And if we know that He hears us, whatever we ask, we know that we have the petitions that we have asked of Him.

RENEWAL THOUGHT
Confidence is infectious. Your faith and confidence will lift those around you.

COURAGE

Gideon was afraid of the enemy. He was full of fear and certainly had a lack of self-worth.

Gideon is scared, weak, under the oppression of the enemy, completely devastated mentally, spiritually, and financially. Yet God sent an angel to call Gideon a mighty man of valor. That means God actually saw him that way, because God does not lie nor does He flatter. God saw His plan for Gideon, and also saw Gideon following it and becoming the way He saw him.

If God says, "You are powerful, fearless, strong, forceful, wealthy, virtuous, and a champion," the humble, submissive, obedient thing to do is say, "Yes, Lord. You are right. You said it, and I believe it."

<u>Blueprint for Life</u>, Casey Treat

Deuteronomy 31:6
Be strong and of good courage, do not fear nor be afraid of them; for the LORD your God, He is the One who goes with you. He will not leave you nor forsake you.

Joshua 1:7-9
Only be strong and very courageous, that you may observe to do according to all the law which Moses My servant commanded you; do not turn from it to the right hand or to the left, that you may prosper wherever you go. This Book of the Law shall not depart from your mouth, but you shall meditate in

it day and night, that you may observe to do according to all that is written in it. For then you will make your way prosperous, and then you will have good success. Have I not commanded you? Be strong and of good courage; do not be afraid, nor be dismayed, for the LORD your God is with you wherever you go.

Judges 6:11-12
Now the Angel of the LORD came and sat under the terebinth tree which was in Ophrah, which belonged to Joash the Abiezrite, while his son Gideon threshed wheat in the winepress, in order to hide it from the Midianites. And the Angel of the LORD appeared to him, and said to him, "The LORD is with you, you mighty man of valor!"

Isaiah 41:13
For I, the LORD your God, will hold your right hand, saying to you, "Fear not, I will help you."

Ephesians 6:10-12
Finally, my brethren, be strong in the Lord and in the power of His might. Put on the whole armor of God, that you may be able to stand against the wiles of the devil. For we do not wrestle against flesh and blood, but against principalities, against powers, against the rulers of the darkness of this age, against spiritual hosts of wickedness in the heavenly places.

Philippians 1:28
And not in any way terrified by your adversaries, which is to them a proof of perdition, but to you of salvation, and that from God.

RENEWAL THOUGHT

Your courage is manifested in your uniqueness. The hero is one who does something the majority doesn't do. Be your own hero today.

DEMONS

There are demon spirits who are real in the world. They know your weaknesses and where you are tempted. They are familiar with your background. That's why they are called familiar spirits. They crawl into your life to give you recurring problems and difficulties. You go through the same things year after year because you let those demons crawl into your life and influence you. Not that you're demon possessed, but you become oppressed and influenced by these demons.

Prayer washes them out. Pray strongly, praying with the Word of God and praying in other tongues in faith. But just because you prayed today doesn't mean it will last for a month because those demons are always crawling back, trying to take over again.

Fighting For Excellence In Leadership, Casey Treat

Matthew 17:14-20

And when they had come to the multitude, a man came to Him, kneeling down to Him and saying, "Lord, have mercy on my son, for he is an epileptic and suffers severely; for he often falls into the fire and often into the water. So I brought him to Your disciples, but they could not cure him." Then Jesus answered and said, "O faithless and perverse generation, how long shall I be with you? How long shall I bear with you? Bring him here to Me." And Jesus rebuked the demon, and it came out of him; and the child was cured from that very hour. Then the disciples came to Jesus privately and said, "Why could we not cast him out?" So Jesus said to them, "Because of your unbelief; for assuredly, I say to you, if you have faith as a mustard seed, you will say to this mountain, 'Move from here to there,' and it will move; and nothing will be impossible for you."

Matthew 18:18
Assuredly, I say to you, whatever you bind on earth will be bound in heaven, and whatever you loose on earth will be loosed in heaven.

Mark 5:1-15
Then they came to the other side of the sea, to the country of the Gadarenes. And when He had come out of the boat, immediately there met Him out of the tombs a man with an unclean spirit, who had his dwelling among the tombs; and no one could bind him, not even with chains, because he had often been bound with shackles and chains. And the chains had been pulled apart by him, and the shackles broken in pieces; neither could anyone tame him. And always, night and day, he was in the mountains and in the tombs, crying out and cutting himself with stones. When he saw Jesus from afar, he ran and worshipped Him. And he cried out with a loud voice and said, "What have I to do with You, Jesus, Son of the Most High God? I implore You by God that You do not torment me." For He said to him, "Come out of the man, unclean spirit!" Then He asked him, "What is your name?" And he answered, saying, "My name is Legion; for we are many." Also he begged Him earnestly that He would not send them out of the country. Now a

large herd of swine was feeding there near the mountains. So all the demons begged Him, saying, "Send us to the swine, that we may enter them." And at once Jesus gave them permission. Then the unclean spirits went out and entered the swine (there were about two thousand); and the herd ran violently down the steep place into the sea, and drowned in the sea. So those who fed the swine fled, and they told it in the city and in the country. And they went out to see what it was that had happened. Then they came to Jesus, and saw the one who had been demon-possessed and had the legion, sitting and clothed and in his right mind. And they were afraid.

Mark 16:17
And these signs will follow those who believe: In My name they will cast out demons; they will speak with new tongues.

Acts 16:16-18
Now it happened, as we went to prayer, that a certain slave girl possessed with a spirit of divination met us, who brought her masters much profit by fortune-telling. This girl followed Paul and us, and cried out, saying, "These men are the servants of the Most High God, who proclaim to us the way of salvation." And this she did for many days. But Paul, greatly annoyed, turned and said to the spirit, "I command you in the name of Jesus Christ to come out of her." And he came out that very hour.

Ephesians 4:27
Nor give place to the devil.

Ephesians 6:10-16

Finally, my brethren, be strong in the Lord and in the power of His might. Put on the whole armor of God, that you may be able to stand against the wiles of the devil. For we do not wrestle against flesh and blood, but against principalities, against powers, against the rulers of the darkness of this age, against spiritual hosts of wickedness in the heavenly places. Therefore take up the whole armor of God, that you may be able to withstand in the evil day, and having done all, to stand. Stand therefore, having girded your waist with truth, having put on the breastplate of righteousness, and having shod your feet with the preparation of the gospel of peace; above all, taking the shield of faith with which you will be able to quench all the fiery darts of the wicked one.

I Peter 5:8-9

Be sober, be vigilant; because your adversary the devil walks about like a roaring lion, seeking whom he may devour. Resist him, steadfast in the faith, knowing that the same sufferings are experienced by your brotherhood in the world.

I John 5:18

We know that whoever is born of God does not sin; but he who has been born of God keeps himself, and the wicked one does not touch him.

RENEWAL THOUGHT

If we will speak the Word daily, the sword of the Spirit will be piercing through every attack of the enemy.

DESIRES

Desire is a God-given force that He uses to help us fulfill our destiny. God knows our personality, our gifts, and our talents. He uses those things and causes us to desire experiences that offer great excitement, fulfillment, and satisfaction.

The desire you feel to speak, to sing, to create, to manage, or to build is there because God placed it there. As you separate your deep, heartfelt desires from your fantasies and ideas, you will be drawn to study and prepare to do those things.

Desire, as God created it, is a positive power. You will discover your destiny as you clarify the things you really want.

<u>Fulfilling Your God-Given Destiny</u>, Casey Treat

Psalm 27:4
One thing I have desired of the LORD, that will I seek: that I may dwell in the house of the LORD all the days of my life, to behold the beauty of the LORD, and to inquire in His temple.

Psalm 37:4
Delight yourself also in the LORD, and He shall give you the desires of your heart.

Proverbs 10:24
The fear of the wicked will come upon him, and the desire of the righteous will be granted.

Proverbs 11:23
The desire of the righteous is only good, but the expectation of the wicked is wrath.

Mark 11:24
Therefore I say to you, whatever things you ask when you pray, believe that you receive them, and you will have them.

John 15:7
If you abide in Me, and My words abide in you, you will ask what you desire, and it shall be done for you.

I Corinthians 14:1
Pursue love, and desire spiritual gifts, but especially that you may prophesy.

1 John 5:14-15
Now this is the confidence that we have in Him, that if we ask anything according to His will, He hears us. And if we know that He hears us, whatever we ask, we know that we have the petitions that we have asked of Him.

RENEWAL THOUGHT
Desire is not only a God-given capacity, it is part of the development of destiny in our lives.

Discipline

Most people lack discipline in their lives because they have no goals, no sense of destiny. They struggle with their weight, for example. Yet when they try to do something about it, their motivation lasts about two weeks - after which there is another piece of exercise equipment piled up in the spare room and another stack of bills for diet programs that didn't work. The problem isn't the equipment or the program. The problem is lack of discipline that comes from no sense of destiny.

If you know your destiny was established by God before the foundation of the world, you have a reason to live life to the fullest and make the most of every moment. When you have a goal, you have the motivation.

It's all a question of "why?" If I have a destiny and a purpose, I have reasons to live right, to stay holy and clean, to pray and study the Word. I have a reason to discipline myself.

Fulfilling Your God-Given Destiny, Casey Treat

Proverbs 10:4
He who has a slack hand becomes poor, but the hand of the diligent makes rich.

Proverbs 11:27
He who earnestly seeks good finds favor, but trouble will come to him who seeks evil.

Proverbs 27:23
Be diligent to know the state of your flocks, and attend to your herds.

I Corinthians 9:27
But I discipline my body and bring it into subjection, lest, when I have preached to others, I myself should become disqualified.

I Timothy 4:12-16
Let no one despise your youth, but be an example to the believers in word, in conduct, in love, in spirit, in faith, in purity. Till I come, give attention to reading, to exhortation, to doctrine. Do not neglect the gift that is in you, which was given to you by prophecy with the laying on of the hands of the eldership. Meditate on these things; give yourself entirely to them, that your progress may be evident to all. Take heed to yourself and to the doctrine. Continue in them, for in doing this you will save both yourself and those who hear you.

II Timothy 1:7
For God has not given us a spirit of fear, but of power and of love and of a sound mind.

II Timothy 2:15
Be diligent to present yourself approved to God, a worker who does not need to be ashamed, rightly dividing the word of truth.

RENEWAL THOUGHT
Discipline that flows out of a sense of destiny is rewarding.

DISCOURAGEMENT

Many of the heroes in the Bible started just like you and me. Most were lowly, insecure, hurt, or frustrated. But they all had something in common: They were searching for their God-given destiny. And to the extent that they believed in themselves and their God, not giving in to negative thoughts, they all discovered and fulfilled their destinies. We assume that biblical figures were "super spiritual." But many struggled with the same human weaknesses we do. Some had low self-esteem. Some felt negative about themselves. Some came from dysfunctional families. Some were born in poverty. Like us, they were bound by insecurities and fears and anxieties. But they heard God and believed what He said about them. As a result, they became people of destiny.

Fulfilling Your God-Given Destiny, Casey Treat

Joshua 1:9
Have I not commanded you? Be strong and of good courage; do not be afraid, nor be dismayed, for the LORD your God is with you wherever you go.

II Kings 6:16
So he answered, "Do not fear, for those who are with us are more than those who are with them."

Isaiah 41:10,13
Fear not, for I am with you; be not dismayed, for I am your God. I will strengthen you, yes, I will help

you, I will uphold you with My righteous right hand. For I, the LORD your God, will hold your right hand, saying to you, "Fear not, I will help you."

Isaiah 43:1
But now, thus says the LORD, who created you, O Jacob, and He who formed you, O Israel: "Fear not, for I have redeemed you; I have called you by your name; you are Mine."

Matthew 10:30
But the very hairs of your head are all numbered.

Matthew 28:5
But the angel answered and said to the women, "Do not be afraid, for I know that you seek Jesus who was crucified."

RENEWAL THOUGHT
If Satan can convince us that our problem is too big and cannot be solved, we are defeated without a fight.

DIVORCE

About half of all marriages go up in smoke because most people do not base their marriages on the Word of God; they base it on how they feel. Their marriage is not based on love or the Word of God or the truth or commitment; therefore, it is going to end up in disaster.

Divorce is clearly not the will of God, but is also not the unpardonable sin. It's not a bigger thing for God to forgive than theft or drinking or smoking or anything else. If you have gone through a divorce, you should not go through guilt and condemnation over it as it's no more difficult for God to forgive that than those other things. In God's eyes it's all the same. The thing that's more complicated about divorce, is that you can change things like smoking a little easier than you can change the things that bring about divorce.

<u>Setting Your Course</u>, Casey Treat

Psalm 103:11-12
For as the heavens are high above the earth, so great is His mercy toward those who fear Him; as far as the east is from the west, so far has He removed our transgressions from us.

Malachi 2:16
"For the LORD God of Israel says that He hates divorce, for it covers one's garment with violence," says the LORD of hosts. "Therefore take heed to your spirit, that you do not deal treacherously."

Matthew 5:31-32

Furthermore it has been said, "Whoever divorces his wife, let him give her a certificate of divorce." But I say to you that whoever divorces his wife for any reason except sexual immorality causes her to commit adultery; and whoever marries a woman who is divorced commits adultery.

Matthew 19:3-11

The Pharisees also came to Him, testing Him, and saying to Him, "Is it lawful for a man to divorce his wife for just any reason?" And He answered and said to them, "Have you not read that He who made them at the beginning 'made them male and female,' and said, 'For this reason a man shall leave his father and mother and be joined to his wife, and the two shall become one flesh'? So then, they are no longer two but one flesh. Therefore what God has joined together, let not man separate." They said to Him, "Why then did Moses command to give a certificate of divorce, and to put her away?" He said to them, "Moses, because of the hardness of your hearts, permitted you to divorce your wives, but from the beginning it was not so. And I say to you, whoever divorces his wife, except for sexual immorality, and marries another, commits adultery; and whoever marries her who is divorced commits adultery." His disciples said to Him, "If such is the case of the man with his wife, it is better not to marry." But He said to them, "All cannot accept this saying, but only those to whom it has been given."

I Corinthians 7:14-15

For the unbelieving husband is sanctified by the wife, and the unbelieving wife is sanctified by the husband; otherwise your children would be unclean, but now they are holy. But if the unbeliever departs, let him depart; a brother or a sister is not under bondage in such cases. But God has called us to peace.

I John 1:9

If we confess our sins, He is faithful and just to forgive us our sins and to cleanse us from all unrighteousness.

RENEWAL THOUGHT

You don't marry the wrong person. When you are married, you are married!

DOUBT

If you are having a problem having faith for something, it is simply because the Word level in your life, in that area, is low.

Some people just can't believe that God would prosper them. It's because they haven't received enough Word about God's prosperity. Some people just can't believe that God wants them healthy. They don't have enough Word to realize the will of God concerning their health. If you get your Word level up, you will get healed. How do you do that? By reading it, by meditating on it. You do that by buying tapes and listening to them, by reading books and studying on it, by going to seminars. When the church door flies open, you fly in. Your faith level will rise up. Why? Because your Word level has risen up.

<u>Setting Your Course</u>, Casey Treat

Matthew 14:28-31
And Peter answered Him and said, "Lord, if it is You, command me to come to You on the water." So He said, "Come." And when Peter had come down out of the boat, he walked on the water to go to Jesus. But when he saw that the wind was boisterous, he was afraid; and beginning to sink he cried out, saying, "Lord, save me!" And immediately Jesus stretched out His hand and caught him, and said to him, "O you of little faith, why did you doubt?"

Matthew 21:21
So Jesus answered and said to them, "Assuredly, I say to you, if you have faith and do not doubt, you will not only do what was done to the fig tree, but also if you say to this mountain, 'Be removed and be cast into the sea,' it will be done."

Mark 11:23
"For assuredly, I say to you, whoever says to this mountain, 'Be removed and be cast into the sea,' and does not doubt in his heart, but believes that those things he says will come to pass, he will have whatever he says."

Luke 12:29
And do not seek what you should eat or what you should drink, nor have an anxious mind.

Romans 14:23
But he who doubts is condemned if he eats, because he does not eat from faith; for whatever is not from faith is sin.

I Timothy 2:8
I desire therefore that the men pray everywhere, lifting up holy hands, without wrath and doubting.

James 1:6-8
But let him ask in faith, with no doubting, for he who doubts is like a wave of the sea driven and tossed by the wind. For let not that man suppose that he will receive anything from the Lord; he is a double-minded man, unstable in all his ways.

RENEWAL THOUGHT

Doubt the voice of doubt and believe the voice of faith.

ETERNAL LIFE

What you earn in sin is death, but the gift of God is eternal life. You can't earn eternal life; you just receive it. You receive that gift from the Lord when you believe in Jesus Christ. When you have faith in Jesus, eternal life is given to you. You become a new person. You have a new life. You are born again! That's what being a Christian is all about.

No one can boast about what good things they've done to get saved. No one can brag about how righteous they are and how much the Lord likes them because of all they've done. All we can do is say, "Thank You Lord for Your grace." All we can do is, by faith, receive what God has done and accept the gift of eternal life through Jesus Christ our Lord. It is the beginning of our relationship with God.

<u>Setting Your Course</u>, Casey Treat

Matthew 25:46
And these will go away into everlasting punishment, but the righteous into eternal life.

John 3:16
For God so loved the world that He gave His only begotten Son, that whoever believes in Him should not perish but have everlasting life.

John 3:36
He who believes in the Son has everlasting life; and

he who does not believe the Son shall not see life, but the wrath of God abides on him.

John 5:24
Most assuredly, I say to you, he who hears My word and believes in Him who sent Me has everlasting life, and shall not come into judgment, but has passed from death into life.

John 14:6
Jesus said to him, "I am the way, the truth, and the life. No one comes to the Father except through Me."

John 17:1-3
Jesus spoke these words, lifted up His eyes to heaven, and said: "Father, the hour has come. Glorify Your Son, that Your Son also may glorify You, as You have given Him authority over all flesh, that He should give eternal life to as many as You have given Him. And this is eternal life, that they may know You, the only true God, and Jesus Christ whom You have sent."

Romans 6:23
For the wages of sin is death, but the gift of God is eternal life in Christ Jesus our Lord.

I Timothy 6:12
Fight the good fight of faith, lay hold on eternal life, to which you were also called and have confessed the good confession in the presence of many witnesses.

I John 1:2
The life was manifested, and we have seen, and bear witness, and declare to you that eternal life which was with the Father and was manifested to us.

I John 2:25
And this is the promise that He has promised us— eternal life.

RENEWAL THOUGHT
If you are not born again, you will die and spend eternity in hell. Spiritual death would be a tragedy if there was not a remedy, but He gave us salvation.

FAITH

What's the first thing that we normally feel like doing? We feel like confessing all our doubts - speaking all our fears - saying everything that probably will go wrong or that ever could go wrong. Our faith is being tested. Are we going to consider this an opportunity to rejoice in the Lord? Are we going to stand firm in the faith knowing that we will come through victoriously?

The trying of our faith is going to produce patience. That's not easy but that's reality. Sometimes the Lord just has to leave us in the oven for awhile. And so God says to us, "There are some things that you're going to have to learn and it will take time. Your faith is going to be tested. But if you will stand and develop patience through this thing, you'll become a wiser and better person."

The Benefits of Godly Wisdom, Casey Treat

Matthew 8:5-10
Now when Jesus had entered Capernaum, a centurion came to Him, pleading with Him, saying, "Lord, my servant is lying at home paralyzed, dreadfully tormented." And Jesus said to him, "I will come and heal him." The centurion answered and said, "Lord, I am not worthy that You should come under my roof. But only speak a word, and my servant will be healed. "For I also am a man under authority, having soldiers under me. And I say to this one, 'Go,' and he goes; and to another, 'Come,' and he comes; and to my servant, 'Do this,' and he does it." When Jesus heard it, He marveled, and

said to those who followed, "Assuredly, I say to you, I have not found such great faith, not even in Israel!"

Matthew 9:22,29
But Jesus turned around, and when He saw her He said, "Be of good cheer, daughter; your faith has made you well." And the woman was made well from that hour. Then He touched their eyes, saying, "According to your faith let it be to you."

Mark 11:22-24
So Jesus answered and said to them, "Have faith in God. For assuredly, I say to you, whoever says to this mountain, 'Be removed and be cast into the sea,' and does not doubt in his heart, but believes that those things he says will come to pass, he will have whatever he says. Therefore I say to you, whatever things you ask when you pray, believe that you receive them, and you will have them."

Romans 1:17
For in it the righteousness of God is revealed from faith to faith; as it is written, "The just shall live by faith."

Romans 4:19-20
And not being weak in faith, he did not consider his own body, already dead (since he was about a hundred years old), and the deadness of Sarah's womb. He did not waver at the promise of God through unbelief, but was strengthened in faith, giving glory to God.

Romans 5:1
Therefore, having been justified by faith, we have peace with God through our Lord Jesus Christ.

Romans 12:3
For I say, through the grace given to me, to everyone who is among you, not to think of himself more highly than he ought to think, but to think soberly, as God has dealt to each one a measure of faith.

II Corinthians 4:13
And since we have the same spirit of faith, according to what is written, "I believed and therefore I spoke," we also believe and therefore speak.

Ephesians 6:16
Above all, taking the shield of faith with which you will be able to quench all the fiery darts of the wicked one.

Hebrews 4:2
For indeed the gospel was preached to us as well as to them; but the word which they heard did not profit them, not being mixed with faith in those who heard it.

Hebrews 11:1,6
Now faith is the substance of things hoped for, the evidence of things not seen. But without faith it is impossible to please Him, for he who comes to God must believe that He is, and that He is a rewarder of those who diligently seek Him.

Hebrews 12:2
. . .looking unto Jesus, the author and finisher of our faith, who for the joy that was set before Him endured the cross, despising the shame, and has sat down at the right of the throne of God.

James 5:15
And the prayer of faith will save the sick, and the Lord will raise him up. And if he has committed sins, he will be forgiven.

RENEWAL THOUGHT
Faith makes your hope a reality.

FEAR

Don't allow fear to hinder you. It is the greatest deception the devil uses against the Christian church.

When the devil tries to hinder you with fear, be wise to it. Don't allow him to convince you of fear. Cast down those imaginations and take those thoughts into captivity.

You might be shaking in your boots, you might stumble over your words, your mouth might be dry as cotton, you might swear, or you might cry. But if you step out in faith, and in obedience to what God has told you to do, you will be victorious the way He says you will. When you act in love, fear cannot remain.

<u>Won By One</u>, Wendy Treat

Job 3:25
For the thing I greatly feared has come upon me, and what I dreaded has happened to me.

Psalm 3:6
I will not be afraid of ten thousands of people who have set themselves against me all around.

Psalm 27:3
Though an army may encamp against me, my heart shall not fear; though war should rise against me, in this I will be confident.

Psalm 91:5
You shall not be afraid of the terror by night, nor of the arrow that flies by day.

Psalm 118:6
The LORD is on my side; I will not fear. What can man do to me?

Proverbs 3:24
When you lie down, you will not be afraid; yes, you will lie down and your sleep will be sweet.

Isaiah 12:2
Behold, God is my salvation, I will trust and not be afraid; "For YAH, the LORD, is my strength and song; he also has become my salvation."

Matthew 6:34
Therefore do not worry about tomorrow, for tomorrow will worry about its own things. Sufficient for the day is its own trouble.

II Timothy 1:7
For God has not given us a spirit of fear, but of power and of love and of a sound mind.

RENEWAL THOUGHT
Keep your mind clear from fear. Let God handle your problems.

FINANCES

Many people are uncomfortable with this idea of Christians having money. And no wonder! The traditional thinking is that if you really want to be spiritual, you should be poor. This error was started in the Dark Ages and created a convoluted religious system that is a blight on both the Church and the world today. Church leaders twisted the concepts of giving and finance so that the churches became massive Cathedrals full of jeweled furniture and incredible treasuries. The people lived in poverty, unaware that they were being robbed by a perverted religious system. Unfortunately, some of this deception continues today.

God has another way, and it has to do with motives. If our desire is pure, to be a blessing, to help others, and to obey God, then God Himself will reward us. . . and reward us openly.

Obviously a reward from God is much better than a reward from men anyway, but the key word is "openly." This means that our reward will be NOW, in this time.

Errors of the Prosperity Gospel, Casey Treat

Deuteronomy 8:18
And you shall remember the LORD your God, for it is He who gives you power to get wealth, that He may establish His covenant which He swore to your fathers, as it is this day.

Psalm 23:5
You prepare a table before me in the presence of

my enemies; you anoint my head with oil; my cup runs over.

Psalm 68:19
Blessed be the Lord, who daily loads us with benefits, the God of our salvation! Selah.

Proverbs 3:9-10
Honor the LORD with your possessions, and with the firstfruits of all your increase; so your barns will be filled with plenty, and your vats will overflow with new wine.

Proverbs 6:31
Yet when he is found, he must restore sevenfold; he may have to give up all the substance of his house.

Proverbs 8:21
That I may cause those who love me to inherit wealth, that I may fill their treasuries.

Malachi 3:8-11
"Will a man rob God? Yet you have robbed Me! But you say, 'In what way have we robbed You?' In tithes and offerings. You are cursed with a curse, for you have robbed Me, even this whole nation. Bring all the tithes into the storehouse, that there may be food in My house, and try Me now in this," says the LORD of hosts, "If I will not open for you the windows of heaven and pour out for you such blessing that there will not be room enough to receive it. And I will rebuke the devourer for your sakes, so that he will not destroy the fruit of your

ground, nor shall the vine fail to bear fruit for you in the field," says the LORD of hosts.

Matthew 14:20
So they all ate and were filled, and they took up twelve baskets full of the fragments that remained.

Luke 6:38
Give, and it will be given to you: good measure, pressed down, shaken together, and running over will be put into your bosom. For with the same measure that you use, it will be measured back to you.

II Corinthians 8:9
For you know the grace of our Lord Jesus Christ, that though He was rich, yet for your sakes He became poor, that you through His poverty might become rich.

Philippians 4:19
And my God shall supply all your need according to His riches in glory by Christ Jesus.

III John 2-3
Beloved, I pray that you may prosper in all things and be in health, just as your soul prospers. For I rejoiced greatly when brethren came and testified of the truth that is in you, just as you walk in the truth.

RENEWAL THOUGHT
What is the first thing you need to do to help the poor? Don't be one of them.

FORGIVENESS

God never intended for us to feel bad or guilty about the past. The Bible says, when you sin, go to God and confess it, and He cleanses you. He forgives you, you are clean from all unrighteousness, and you are right back to that original perfect position: blameless, holy, and righteous with God.

Casey Treat

Psalm 103:3
Who forgives all your iniquities, who heals all your diseases.

Isaiah 43:18-19
Do not remember the former things, nor consider the things of old. Behold, I will do a new thing, now it shall spring forth; shall you not know it? I will even make a road in the wilderness and rivers in the desert.

Matthew 6:14
For if you forgive men their trespasses, your heavenly Father will also forgive you.

Mark 11:25-26
And whenever you stand praying, if you have anything against anyone, forgive him, that your Father in heaven may also forgive you your trespasses. But if you do not forgive, neither will your Father in heaven forgive your trespasses.

Luke 6:37
Judge not, and you shall not be judged. Condemn not, and you shall not be condemned. Forgive, and you will be forgiven.

Luke 7:47
Therefore I say to you, her sins, which are many, are forgiven, for she loved much. But to whom little is forgiven, the same loves little.

Ephesians 1:7
In Him we have redemption through His blood, the forgiveness of sins, according to the riches of His grace.

Ephesians 4:32
And be kind to one another, tenderhearted, forgiving one another, just as God in Christ forgave you.

Philippians 3:13-14
Brethren, I do not count myself to have apprehended; but one thing I do, forgetting those things which are behind and reaching forward to those things which are ahead, I press toward the goal for the prize of the upward call of God in Christ Jesus.

Colossians 3:13
Bearing with one another, and forgiving one another, if anyone has a complaint against another; even as Christ forgave you, so you also must do.

I John 1:9
If we confess our sins, He is faithful and just to forgive us our sins and to cleanse us from all unrighteousness.

RENEWAL THOUGHT
When you love yourself, you confess your sin, repent of it, get cleansed from it, and go on about your business praising God.

Friendship

Each one of us, whether we want to admit it or not, is part of a body. And, just as in the physical body, one part can do little without the other parts. As a part, you can be strong and effective. If you separate yourself from other parts of the body, you will accomplish little, enjoy little, and not have the life you desire.

<u>Being Spiritually Minded</u>, Casey Treat

Proverbs 17:17
A friend loves at all times, and a brother is born for adversity.

Proverbs 18:24
A man who has friends must himself be friendly, but there is a friend who sticks closer than a brother.

John 15:13-15
Greater love has no one than this, than to lay down one's life for his friends. You are My friends if you do whatever I command you. No longer do I call you servants, for a servant does not know what his master is doing; but I have called you friends, for all things that I heard from My Father I have made known to you.

James 2:23
And the Scripture was fulfilled which says, "Abraham believed God, and it was accounted to him for righteousness." And he was called the friend of God.

James 4:4

Adulterers and adulteresses! Do you not know that friendship with the world is enmity with God? Whoever therefore wants to be a friend of the world makes himself an enemy of God.

RENEWAL THOUGHT

You are not a hermit or an "island unto yourself." You need God, and you need friends.

GIVING

The world was created to function on the seed principle. When man tries to avoid or ignore this principle, he will always suffer. The farmer knows there is no harvest without first planting seed; the same principle applies in our lives in everything we do.

<u>Keys to Life</u>, Casey Treat

Proverbs 3:9-10
Honor the LORD with your possessions, and with the firstfruits of all your increase; so your barns will be filled with plenty, and your vats will overflow with new wine.

Proverbs 11:24-25
There is one who scatters, yet increases more; and there is one who withholds more than is right, but it leads to poverty. The generous soul will be made rich, and he who waters will also be watered himself.

Proverbs 21:25-26
The desire of the lazy man kills him, for his hands refuse to labor. He covets greedily all day long, but the righteous gives and does not spare.

Malachi 3:8-11
"Will a man rob God? Yet you have robbed Me! But you say, 'In what way have we robbed You?' In tithes and offerings. You are cursed with a curse, for you have robbed Me, even this whole nation.

Bring all the tithes into the storehouse, that there may be food in My house, and try Me now in this," says the LORD of hosts, "If I will not open for you the windows of heaven and pour out for you such blessing that there will not be room enough to receive it. And I will rebuke the devourer for your sakes, so that he will not destroy the fruit of your ground, nor shall the vine fail to bear fruit for you in the field," says the LORD of hosts.

Mark 10:29-30

So Jesus answered and said, "Assuredly, I say to you, there is no one who has left house or brothers or sisters or father or mother or wife or children or lands, for My sake and the gospel's, who shall not receive a hundredfold now in this time— houses and brothers and sisters and mothers and children and lands, with persecutions— and in the age to come, eternal life."

Luke 6:38

Give, and it will be given to you: good measure, pressed down, shaken together, and running over will be put into your bosom. For with the same measure that you use, it will be measured back to you.

II Corinthians 8:9

For you know the grace of our Lord Jesus Christ, that though He was rich, yet for your sakes He became poor, that you through His poverty might become rich.

II Corinthians 9:6-8
But this I say: He who sows sparingly will also reap sparingly, and he who sows bountifully will also reap bountifully. So let each one give as he purposes in his heart, not grudgingly or of necessity; for God loves a cheerful giver. And God is able to make all grace abound toward you, that you, always having all sufficiency in all things, may have an abundance for every good work.

Galatians 6:7-10
Do not be deceived, God is not mocked; for whatever a man sows, that he will also reap. For he who sows to his flesh will of the flesh reap corruption, but he who sows to the Spirit will of the Spirit reap everlasting life. And let us not grow weary while doing good, for in due season we shall reap if we do not lose heart. Therefore, as we have opportunity, let us do good to all, especially to those who are of the household of faith.

III John 2
Beloved, I pray that you may prosper in all things and be in health, just as your soul prospers.

RENEWAL THOUGHT
Giving is the source of life.

GOD'S FAITHFULNESS

Hebrews 2:17 says: "Therefore, in all things He had to be made like His brethren, that He might be a merciful and faithful High Priest in things pertaining to God, to make propitiation for the sins of the people." Jesus' high-priestly ministry is to be always making intercession for us. He is a high priest today for you and me, and the Bible says that He is a compassionate high priest. He is a loving high priest. The same love that He moved in when He walked this earth, healed the sick, raised the dead, and fed poor people, is flowing through Him today as a high priest for you and me. He is a helper, an advocate, and an assistant to you and me, and He is a compassionate high priest.

Was Jesus a healer yesterday? Then He is a healer today, and He'll be a healer tomorrow. Did He give to the poor yesterday? Then He'll give to the poor today, and tomorrow. Was Jesus a lover yesterday? Then He'll be a lover tomorrow.

Casey Treat

Deuteronomy 7:9
Therefore know that the LORD your God, He is God, the faithful God who keeps covenant and mercy for a thousand generations with those who love Him and keep His commandments.

I Kings 8:56
Blessed be the LORD, who has given rest to His people Israel, according to all that He promised.

There has not failed one word of all His good promise, which He promised through His servant Moses.

Psalm 36:5
Your mercy, O LORD, is in the heavens; your faithfulness reaches to the clouds.

Psalm 89:1
I will sing of the mercies of the LORD forever; with my mouth will I make known Your faithfulness to all generations.

Matthew 28:18-20
And Jesus came and spoke to them, saying, "All authority has been given to Me in heaven and on earth. Go therefore and make disciples of all the nations, baptizing them in the name of the Father and of the Son and of the Holy Spirit, teaching them to observe all things that I have commanded you; and lo, I am with you always, even to the end of the age." Amen.

I Corinthians 1:9
God is faithful, by whom you were called into the fellowship of His Son, Jesus Christ our Lord.

II Thessalonians 3:3
But the Lord is faithful, who will establish you and guard you from the evil one.

Hebrews 10:23
Let us hold fast the confession of our hope without wavering, for He who promised is faithful.

Hebrews 13:5,8
Let your conduct be without covetousness; be content with such things as you have. For He Himself has said, "I will never leave you nor forsake you." Jesus Christ is the same yesterday, today, and forever.

RENEWAL THOUGHT

God's plan at the beginning is the same as God's plan at the end.

GOD'S LOVE

God's love is still here today. God is still God. God is the same yesterday, today, and forever. The love of God never changes. The love of God is still being manifested on the earth. God's love is still being poured out to all people. Whoever will receive God's love will receive His power because love is the super power of God.

Casey Treat

II Chronicles 5:13-14
Indeed it came to pass, when the trumpeters and singers were as one, to make one sound to be heard in praising and thanking the LORD, and when they lifted up their voice with the trumpets and cymbals and instruments of music, and praised the LORD, saying: "For He is good, for His mercy endures forever," that the house, the house of the LORD, was filled with a cloud, so that the priests could not continue ministering because of the cloud; for the glory of the LORD filled the house of God.

Psalms 136:1-4
Oh, give thanks to the LORD, for He is good! For His mercy endures forever. Oh, give thanks to the God of gods! For His mercy endures forever. Oh, give thanks to the Lord of lords! For His mercy endures forever. To Him who alone does great wonders, for His mercy endures forever.

John 3:16

For God so loved the world that He gave His only begotten Son, that whoever believes in Him should not perish but have everlasting life.

John 15:9-10

As the Father loved Me, I also have loved you; abide in My love. If you keep My commandments, you will abide in My love, just as I have kept My Father's commandments and abide in His love.

Romans 5:5,8

Now hope does not disappoint, because the love of God has been poured out in our hearts by the Holy Spirit who was given to us. But God demonstrates His own love toward us, in that while we were still sinners, Christ died for us.

Romans 8:35-39

Who shall separate us from the love of Christ? Shall tribulation, or distress, or persecution, or famine, or nakedness, or peril, or sword? As it is written: "For Your sake we are killed all day long; we are accounted as sheep for the slaughter." Yet in all these things we are more than conquerors through Him who loved us. For I am persuaded that neither death nor life, nor angels nor principalities nor powers, nor things present nor things to come, nor height nor depth, nor any other created thing, shall be able to separate us from the love of God which is in Christ Jesus our Lord.

I John 4:7-12,18

Beloved, let us love one another, for love is of God; and everyone who loves is born of God and knows God. He who does not love does not know God, for God is love. In this the love of God was manifested toward us, that God has sent His only begotten Son into the world, that we might live through Him. In this is love, not that we loved God, but that He loved us and sent His Son to be the propitiation for our sins. Beloved, if God so loved us, we also ought to love one another. No one has seen God at any time. If we love one another, God abides in us, and His love has been perfected in us. There is no fear in love; but perfect love casts out fear, because fear involves torment. But he who fears has not been made perfect in love.

RENEWAL THOUGHT

God loves us unconditionally with all that He is and all that He has.

GOVERNMENT

God gives us leaders in government to keep order and safety in our society. We must pray for them and support them positively. Let's do our part to influence our government with the Spirit of God.

Casey Treat

Psalm 22:28
For the kingdom is the LORD'S, and He rules over the nations.

Proverbs 8:15-16
By me kings reign, and rulers decree justice. By me princes rule, and nobles, all the judges of the earth.

Proverbs 21:1
The king's heart is in the hand of the LORD, like the rivers of water; he turns it wherever He wishes.

Matthew 22:17-21
"Tell us, therefore, what do You think? Is it lawful to pay taxes to Caesar, or not?" But Jesus perceived their wickedness, and said, "Why do you test Me, you hypocrites? Show Me the tax money." So they brought Him a denarius. And He said to them, "Whose image and inscription is this?" They said to Him, "Caesar's." And He said to them, "Render therefore to Caesar the things that are Caesar's, and to God the things that are God's."

Romans 13:1-7
Let every soul be subject to the governing authorities. For there is no authority except from God, and the authorities that exist are appointed by God. Therefore whoever resists the authority resists the ordinance of God, and those who resist will bring judgment on themselves. For rulers are not a terror to good works, but to evil. Do you want to be unafraid of the authority? Do what is good, and you will have praise from the same. For he is God's minister to you for good. But if you do evil, be afraid; for he does not bear the sword in vain; for he is God's minister, an avenger to execute wrath on him who practices evil. Therefore you must be subject, not only because of wrath but also for conscience' sake. For because of this you also pay taxes, for they are God's ministers attending continually to this very thing. Render therefore to all their due: taxes to whom taxes are due, customs to whom customs, fear to whom fear, honor to whom honor.

I Timothy 2:1-2
Therefore I exhort first of all that supplications, prayers, intercessions, and giving of thanks be made for all men, for kings and all who are in authority, that we may lead a quiet and peaceable life in all godliness and reverence.

Titus 3:1
Remind them to be subject to rulers and authorities, to obey, to be ready for every good work.

I Peter 2:13-17

Therefore submit yourselves to every ordinance of man for the Lord's sake, whether to the king as supreme, or to governors, as to those who are sent by him for the punishment of evildoers and for the praise of those who do good. For this is the will of God, that by doing good you may put to silence the ignorance of foolish men—as free, yet not using liberty as a cloak for vice, but as bondservants of God. Honor all people. Love the brotherhood. Fear God. Honor the king.

RENEWAL THOUGHT
Government is of God - be a positive part of it.

97

GRACE

Remember that we did not earn either salvation or the right to be filled with the Holy Ghost. We did not earn being the beautiful Christian people that we are. God gave that to us as a free gift. We are saved because God gave us salvation; not because we have earned anything.

What you have done or are doing, does not have anything to do with how to get born again. Teaching that, in order to be born again, you must confess all your sins out of you, is wrong. The foundation for that kind of teaching and ministry is one of works. "You have to work your way to Heaven. You must confess everything out so that you can work your way to God." We cannot earn anything from God. We have earned zero of what God has given us. It is by God's grace alone that we are saved when we make Jesus our Lord.

Won By One, Wendy Treat

Psalm 145:8-9
The LORD is gracious and full of compassion, slow to anger and great in mercy. The LORD is good to all, and His tender mercies are over all His works.

John 1:14,16-17
And the Word became flesh and dwelt among us, and we beheld His glory, the glory as of the only begotten of the Father, full of grace and truth. And of His fullness we have all received, and grace for grace. For the law was given through Moses, but grace and truth came through Jesus Christ.

Romans 3:24
Being justified freely by His grace through the redemption that is in Christ Jesus.

Romans 5:20-21
Moreover the law entered that the offense might abound. But where sin abounded, grace abounded much more, so that as sin reigned in death, even so grace might reign through righteousness to eternal life through Jesus Christ our Lord.

II Corinthians 8:9
For you know the grace of our Lord Jesus Christ, that though He was rich, yet for your sakes He became poor, that you through His poverty might become rich.

II Corinthians 9:8
And God is able to make all grace abound toward you, that you, always having all sufficiency in all things, may have an abundance for every good work.

II Corinthians 12:9
And He said to me, "My grace is sufficient for you, for My strength is made perfect in weakness." Therefore most gladly I will rather boast in my infirmities, that the power of Christ may rest upon me.

Ephesians 1:2-7
Grace to you and peace from God our Father and the Lord Jesus Christ. Blessed be the God and Father of our Lord Jesus Christ, who has blessed us with every spiritual blessing in the heavenly places

in Christ, just as He chose us in Him before the foundation of the world, that we should be holy and without blame before Him in love, having predestined us to adoption as sons by Jesus Christ to Himself, according to the good pleasure of His will, to the praise of the glory of His grace, by which He has made us accepted in the Beloved. In Him we have redemption through His blood, the forgiveness of sins, according to the riches of His grace.

Ephesians 2:6-9
And raised us up together, and made us sit together in the heavenly places in Christ Jesus, that in the ages to come He might show the exceeding riches of His grace in His kindness toward us in Christ Jesus. For by grace you have been saved through faith, and that not of yourselves; it is the gift of God, not of works, lest anyone should boast.

Hebrews 4:16
Let us therefore come boldly to the throne of grace, that we may obtain mercy and find grace to help in time of need.

James 4:6
But He gives more grace. Therefore He says: "God resists the proud, but gives grace to the humble."

II Peter 1:2
Grace and peace be multiplied to you in the knowledge of God and of Jesus our Lord.

RENEWAL THOUGHT
We are to be simply vessels for God's grace to show through.

GROWING UP
SPIRITUALLY

Church! Wake up! Plug in! If we will walk in the knowledge of God, the understanding of God and the wisdom of God, no matter how dark it is around us, we will shine with the light of heaven. But we've got to be serious about knowing God and having the thoughts of God. We've got to make them a part of our life every day. We should have a biblical reason for everything we do, and if we don't have a biblical reason, we probably shouldn't be doing it.

That's why we talk different. We can't talk like the world to describe the things of God. We talk like spiritual people because we're talking about spiritual things. The people in the world don't get it. When they first come into the church it's almost like a foreign language. But if they're hungry and desire to know God, pretty soon they begin to click in. Pretty soon they start to get understanding because the Holy Spirit is revealing the things that God has prepared for them.

<u>The Benefits of Godly Wisdom</u>, Casey Treat

Mark 4:14,20,26-29
The sower sows the word. But these are the ones sown on good ground, those who hear the word, accept it, and bear fruit: some thirtyfold, some sixty, and some a hundred. And He said, "The kingdom of God is as if a man should scatter seed on the ground, and should sleep by night and rise by day,

and the seed should sprout and grow, he himself does not know how. For the earth yields crops by itself: first the blade, then the head, after that the full grain in the head. But when the grain ripens, immediately he puts in the sickle, because the harvest has come."

Romans 10:17
So then faith comes by hearing, and hearing by the word of God.

Romans 12:2
And do not be conformed to this world, but be transformed by the renewing of your mind, that you may prove what is that good and acceptable and perfect will of God.

I Corinthians 3:1-3
And I, brethren, could not speak to you as to spiritual people but as to carnal, as to babes in Christ. I fed you with milk and not with solid food; for until now you were not able to receive it, and even now you are still not able; for you are still carnal. For where there are envy, strife, and divisions among you, are you not carnal and behaving like mere men?

I Corinthians 14:20
Brethren, do not be children in understanding; however, in malice be babes, but in understanding be mature.

Ephesians 4:11-15
And He Himself gave some to be apostles, some prophets, some evangelists, and some pastors and

teachers, for the equipping of the saints for the work of ministry, for the edifying of the body of Christ, till we all come to the unity of the faith and of the knowledge of the Son of God, to a perfect man, to the measure of the stature of the fullness of Christ; that we should no longer be children, tossed to and fro and carried about with every wind of doctrine, by the trickery of men, in the cunning craftiness of deceitful plotting, but, speaking the truth in love, may grow up in all things into Him who is the head— Christ.

II Thessalonians 1:3
We are bound to thank God always for you, brethren, as it is fitting, because your faith grows exceedingly, and the love of every one of you all abounds toward each other.

II Timothy 2:15
Be diligent to present yourself approved to God, a worker who does not need to be ashamed, rightly dividing the word of truth.

Hebrews 5:12-14
For though by this time you ought to be teachers, you need someone to teach you again the first principles of the oracles of God; and you have come to need milk and not solid food. For everyone who partakes only of milk is unskilled in the word of righteousness, for he is a babe. But solid food belongs to those who are of full age, that is, those who by reason of use have their senses exercised to discern both good and evil.

Hebrews 6:1-3
Therefore, leaving the discussion of the elementary principles of Christ, let us go on to perfection, not laying again the foundation of repentance from dead works and of faith toward God, of the doctrine of baptisms, of laying on of hands, of resurrection of the dead, and of eternal judgment. And this we will do if God permits.

I Peter 2:1-2
Therefore, laying aside all malice, all guile, hypocrisy, envy, and all evil speaking, as newborn babes, desire the pure milk of the word, that you may grow thereby.

RENEWAL THOUGHT
To be born again is just that, you are born. Now, just like a baby, you must grow up.

Healing

Jesus was sent by the Father to undo what Satan had done, and that includes overcoming sickness and disease. In Genesis 3, Satan came and brought spiritual death. Jesus came to undo that by bringing spiritual life. Satan caused their bodies to decay and die. Jesus came to undo that. When you make Jesus your Lord, you will eventually have a glorified body, a spiritual body that decays no more and will live forever. When Satan came in he brought sickness and disease. Jesus bore that sickness and disease so you no longer have to bear it in your own body.

Setting Your Course, Casey Treat

Exodus 15:26
And said, "If you diligently heed the voice of the LORD your God and do what is right in His sight, give ear to His commandments and keep all His statutes, I will put none of the diseases on you which I have brought on the Egyptians. For I am the LORD who heals you."

Psalm 103:3
Who forgives all your iniquities, who heals all your diseases.

Psalm 107:20
He sent His word and healed them, and delivered them from their destructions.

Matthew 4:23
And Jesus went about all Galilee, teaching in their synagogues, preaching the gospel of the kingdom, and healing all kinds of sickness and all kinds of disease among the people.

Matthew 9:35
Then Jesus went about all the cities and villages, teaching in their synagogues, preaching the gospel of the kingdom, and healing every sickness and every disease among the people.

Matthew 10:1
And when He had called His twelve disciples to Him, He gave them power over unclean spirits, to cast them out, and to heal all kinds of sickness and all kinds of disease.

Mark 16:17-18
And these signs will follow those who believe: In My name they will cast out demons; they will speak with new tongues; they will take up serpents; and if they drink anything deadly, it will by no means hurt them; they will lay hands on the sick, and they will recover.

Luke 9:11
But when the multitudes knew it, they followed Him; and He received them and spoke to them about the kingdom of God, and healed those who had need of healing.

Acts 5:16

Also a multitude gathered from the surrounding cities to Jerusalem, bringing sick people and those who were tormented by unclean spirits, and they were all healed.

Acts 10:38

How God anointed Jesus of Nazareth with the Holy Spirit and with power, who went about doing good and healing all who were oppressed by the devil, for God was with Him.

James 5:15-16

And the prayer of faith will save the sick, and the Lord will raise him up. And if he has committed sins, he will be forgiven. Confess your trespasses to one another, and pray for one another, that you may be healed. The effective, fervent prayer of a righteous man avails much.

I Peter 2:24

Who Himself bore our sins in His own body on the tree, that we, having died to sins, might live for righteousness— by whose stripes you were healed.

III John 2

Beloved, I pray that you may prosper in all things and be in health, just as your soul prospers.

RENEWAL THOUGHT

God created you to prosper and be healthy, not struggle through life sick and poor.

HEALTH

III John 2 says that, when your soul is prosperous, and is renewed to the Word of God, you will prosper and live in health. Divine health is for those who have been transformed by renewing their minds, and that's better than divine healing. I'd rather live in divine health than be divinely healed. If I'm in divine health, I never need healing.

Casey Treat

Genesis 43:28
And they answered, "Your servant our father is in good health; he is still alive." And they bowed their heads down and prostrated themselves.

Proverbs 4:20-22
My son, give attention to my words; incline your ear to my sayings. Do not let them depart from your eyes; keep them in the midst of your heart; for they are life to those who find them, and health to all their flesh.

Proverbs 13:17
A wicked messenger falls into trouble, but a faithful ambassador brings health.

Proverbs 16:24
Pleasant words are like a honeycomb, sweetness to the soul and health to the bones.

Exodus 15:26
And said, "If you diligently heed the voice of the LORD your God and do what is right in His sight, give ear to His commandments and keep all His statutes, I will put none of the diseases on you which I have brought on the Egyptians. For I am the LORD who heals you."

RENEWAL THOUGHT
Our health should show the goodness of God.

Heaven

Through Jesus we are on our way to heaven, but heaven is not our goal. Obeying and pleasing the Lord, fulfilling destiny is our goal. We can live with heaven on earth if we obey the will of the Lord.

Casey Treat

Genesis 1:1
In the beginning God created the heavens and the earth.

John 3:13
No one has ascended to heaven but He who came down from heaven, that is, the Son of Man who is in heaven.

John 14:1-4
Let not your heart be troubled; you believe in God, believe also in Me. In My Father's house are many mansions; if it were not so, I would have told you. I go to prepare a place for you. And if I go and prepare a place for you, I will come again and receive you to Myself; that where I am, there you may be also. And where I go you know, and the way you know.

II Corinthians 5:8
We are confident, yes, well pleased rather to be absent from the body and to be present with the Lord.

Philippians 3:20

For our citizenship is in heaven, from which we also eagerly wait for the Savior, the Lord Jesus Christ.

I Peter 1:3-4

Blessed be the God and Father of our Lord Jesus Christ, who according to His abundant mercy has begotten us again to a living hope through the resurrection of Jesus Christ from the dead, to an inheritance incorruptible and undefiled and that does not fade away, reserved in heaven for you.

Revelation 21:1-4

Now I saw a new heaven and a new earth, for the first heaven and the first earth had passed away. Also there was no more sea. Then I, John, saw the holy city, New Jerusalem, coming down out of heaven from God, prepared as a bride adorned for her husband. And I heard a loud voice from heaven saying, "Behold, the tabernacle of God is with men, and He will dwell with them, and they shall be His people. God Himself will be with them and be their God. And God will wipe away every tear from their eyes; there shall be no more death, nor sorrow, nor crying. There shall be no more pain, for the former things have passed away."

Revelation 21:10-27

And he carried me away in the Spirit to a great and high mountain, and showed me the great city, the holy Jerusalem, descending out of heaven from God, having the glory of God. Her light was like a most precious stone, like a jasper stone, clear as crystal. Also she had a great and high wall with twelve gates, and twelve angels at the gates, and names written on them, which are the names of the twelve tribes of the children of Israel: three gates on the east, three gates on the north, three gates on the south, and three gates on the west. Now the wall of the city had twelve foundations, and on them were the names of the twelve apostles of the Lamb. And he who talked with me had a gold reed to measure the city, its gates, and its wall. The city is laid out as a square; its length is as great as its breadth. And he measured the city with the reed: twelve thousand furlongs. Its length, breadth, and height are equal. Then he measured its wall: one hundred and forty-four cubits, according to the measure of a man, that is, of an angel. The construction of its wall was of jasper; and the city was pure gold, like clear glass. The foundations of the wall of the city were adorned with all kinds of precious stones: the first foundation was jasper, the second sapphire, the third chalcedony, the fourth emerald, the fifth sardonyx, the sixth sardius, the seventh chrysolite, the eighth beryl, the ninth topaz, the tenth chrysoprase, the eleventh jacinth, and the twelfth amethyst. The twelve gates were twelve pearls: each individual gate was of one pearl. And the street of the city was pure gold, like transparent glass. But I saw no temple in it, for the Lord God Almighty and the Lamb are its temple. The city had no need of the sun or of the moon to shine in it, for the glory of God illuminated it. The Lamb is its light. And the nations of those who are saved shall walk in its light, and the kings of the earth bring their glory and honor into it. Its gates shall not be shut at all by day (there shall be no night there). And they shall bring the glory and the honor of the nations into it. But there shall by no means enter it anything that defiles, or causes an abomination or a lie, but only those who are written in the Lamb's Book of Life.

RENEWAL THOUGHT

Heaven is the launching pad for the next plan of God for our lives.

Hell

There are two spiritual kingdoms at work in the earth today: the kingdom of God and the kingdom of the devil. These two kingdoms are very real, and they are all around us right now. Both kingdoms are suffering violence. Both are aggressively, violently going after people. The kingdom of the devil is attempting to consume our world with compromise, evil, and negativity. He's aggressively attacking in the area of politics, social life, and in family life. In all these areas, the devil is trying to possess the lives of people and he's making some progress in many cases.

Whichever kingdom you side with will affect your life. If you fight to hang on to your old ways of thinking - your television programs, your worldly music, your loose morals - the kingdom of the devil will control your life even as a Christian. He will keep depression, poverty and disease upon you. He will bring divorce into your home and tear your family apart. The kingdom of the devil will force these things on you unless you fight for the kingdom of God.

<u>Fighting For Excellence In Leadership</u>, Casey Treat

Matthew 10:28
And do not fear those who kill the body but cannot kill the soul. But rather fear Him who is able to destroy both soul and body in hell.

Matthew 16:18
And I also say to you that you are Peter, and on this rock I will build My church, and the gates of Hades shall not prevail against it.

Matthew 25:30
And cast the unprofitable servant into the outer darkness. There will be weeping and gnashing of teeth.

Luke 16:19-31
There was a certain rich man who was clothed in purple and fine linen and fared sumptuously every day. But there was a certain beggar named Lazarus, full of sores, who was laid at his gate, desiring to be fed with the crumbs which fell from the rich man's table. Moreover the dogs came and licked his sores. So it was that the beggar died, and was carried by the angels to Abraham's bosom. The rich man also died and was buried. And being in torments in Hades, he lifted up his eyes and saw Abraham afar off, and Lazarus in his bosom. Then he cried and said, "Father Abraham, have mercy on me, and send Lazarus that he may dip the tip of his finger in water and cool my tongue; for I am tormented in this flame." But Abraham said, "Son, remember that in your lifetime you received your good things, and likewise Lazarus evil things; but now he is comforted and you are tormented. And besides all this, between us and you there is a great gulf fixed, so that those who want to pass from here to you cannot, nor can those from there pass to us." Then he said, "I beg you therefore, father, that you would send him to my father's house, for I have

five brothers, that he may testify to them, lest they also come to this place of torment." Abraham said to him, "They have Moses and the prophets; let them hear them." And he said, "No, father Abraham; but if one goes to them from the dead, they will repent." But he said to him, "If they do not hear Moses and the prophets, neither will they be persuaded though one rise from the dead."

Acts 2:26-27,31

Therefore my heart rejoiced, and my tongue was glad; moreover my flesh also will rest in hope. For You will not leave my soul in Hades, nor will You allow Your Holy One to see corruption. You have made known to me the ways of life; you will make me full of joy in Your presence. Men and brethren, let me speak freely to you of the patriarch David, that he is both dead and buried, and his tomb is with us to this day. Therefore, being a prophet, and knowing that God had sworn with an oath to him that of the fruit of his body, according to the flesh, He would raise up the Christ to sit on his throne, he, foreseeing this, spoke concerning the resurrection of the Christ, that His soul was not left in Hades, nor did His flesh see corruption.

II Peter 2:4-9

For if God did not spare the angels who sinned, but cast them down to hell and delivered them into chains of darkness, to be reserved for judgment; and did not spare the ancient world, but saved Noah, one of eight people, a preacher of righteousness, bringing in the flood on the world of the ungodly;

and turning the cities of Sodom and Gomorrah into ashes, condemned them to destruction, making them an example to those who afterward would live ungodly; and delivered righteous Lot, who was oppressed by the filthy conduct of the wicked (for that righteous man, dwelling among them, tormented his righteous soul from day to day by seeing and hearing their lawless deeds)—then the Lord knows how to deliver the godly out of temptations and to reserve the unjust under punishment for the day of judgment.

Revelation 1:18
I am He who lives, and was dead, and behold, I am alive forevermore. Amen. And I have the keys of Hades and of Death.

Revelation 20:12-14
And I saw the dead, small and great, standing before God, and books were opened. And another book was opened, which is the Book of Life. And the dead were judged according to their works, by the things which were written in the books. The sea gave up the dead who were in it, and Death and Hades delivered up the dead who were in them. And they were judged, each one according to his works. Then Death and Hades were cast into the lake of fire. This is the second death.

RENEWAL THOUGHT
Every person that has gone to hell in the last 2,000 years thought about getting born again because everyone that goes there had a chance to avoid it.

HOPE

A person who is renewing their mind to the Bible is optimistic. They have faith, and they have hope. Faith and hope work together, because faith is the substance, the tangibility of what you are hoping for.

By faith, and with hope, you see things other people can't see. It's the evidence of what you can't see. With a renewed mind, you have a good report.

Casey Treat

Psalm 9:18
For the needy shall not always be forgotten; the expectation of the poor shall not perish forever.

Psalm 31:24
Be of good courage, and He shall strengthen your heart, all you who hope in the LORD.

Psalm 33:18,22
Behold, the eye of the LORD is on those who fear Him, on those who hope in His mercy. . . Let Your mercy, O LORD, be upon us, just as we hope in You.

Psalm 43:5
Why are you cast down, O my soul? And why are you disquieted within me? Hope in God; for I shall yet praise Him, the help of my countenance and my God.

Psalm 71:5
For You are my hope, O Lord GOD; you are my trust from my youth.

Proverbs 10:28
The hope of the righteous will be gladness, but the expectation of the wicked will perish.

Proverbs 13:12
Hope deferred makes the heart sick, but when the desire comes, it is a tree of life.

Proverbs 14:32
The wicked is banished in his wickedness, but the righteous has a refuge in his death.

Romans 4:18-21
Who, contrary to hope, in hope believed, so that he became the father of many nations, according to what was spoken, "So shall your descendants be." And not being weak in faith, he did not consider his own body, already dead (since he was about a hundred years old), and the deadness of Sarah's womb. He did not waver at the promise of God through unbelief, but was strengthened in faith, giving glory to God, and being fully convinced that what He had promised He was also able to perform.

Romans 5:1-5
Therefore, having been justified by faith, we have peace with God through our Lord Jesus Christ, through whom also we have access by faith into this grace in which we stand, and rejoice in hope of

the glory of God. And not only that, but we also glory in tribulations, knowing that tribulation produces perseverance; and perseverance, character; and character, hope. Now hope does not disappoint, because the love of God has been poured out in our hearts by the Holy Spirit who was given to us.

Romans 12:12
Rejoicing in hope, patient in tribulation, continuing steadfastly in prayer.

I Corinthians 13:13
And now abide faith, hope, love, these three; but the greatest of these is love.

Ephesians 2:12
That at that time you were without Christ, being aliens from the commonwealth of Israel and strangers from the covenants of promise, having no hope and without God in the world.

Colossians 1:27
To them God willed to make known what are the riches of the glory of this mystery among the Gentiles: which is Christ in you, the hope of glory.

I Thessalonians 5:8
But let us who are of the day be sober, putting on the breastplate of faith and love, and as a helmet the hope of salvation.

Titus 1:2
In hope of eternal life which God, who cannot lie, promised before time began.

Titus 2:13
Looking for the blessed hope and glorious appearing of our great God and Savior Jesus Christ.

Hebrews 11:1
Now faith is the substance of things hoped for, the evidence of things not seen.

1 Peter 1:3
Blessed be the God and Father of our Lord Jesus Christ, who according to His abundant mercy has begotten us again to a living hope through the resurrection of Jesus Christ from the dead.

I John 3:3
And everyone who has this hope in Him purifies himself, just as He is pure.

RENEWAL THOUGHT
Hope is the anchor of your soul.

HUSBANDS

The spiritual and emotional condition of your wife and children are your responsibility. Before we started Christian Faith Center, we would watch the wives of the guest speakers at our church. We could always tell what was really happening by just watching them. Anybody can put together a good show for a service. You can memorize a sermon and have your jokes down pretty well. You can go through the service routine, but if your wife is sitting there depressed, you know what you're saying is not real. You may bless some folks, but if your wife isn't doing well, then you know you are not right.

<u>Leading People in Church Growth</u>, Casey Treat

Genesis 2:23-24
And Adam said: "This is now bone of my bones and flesh of my flesh; she shall be called Woman, because she was taken out of Man." Therefore a man shall leave his father and mother and be joined to his wife, and they shall become one flesh.

Proverbs 5:18
Let your fountain be blessed, and rejoice with the wife of your youth.

Proverbs 18:22
He who finds a wife finds a good thing, and obtains favor from the LORD.

Ecclesiastes 9:9
Live joyfully with the wife whom you love all the days of your vain life which He has given you under the sun, all your days of vanity; for that is your portion in life, and in the labor which you perform under the sun.

Ephesians 5:21-23,28-29,31,33
Submitting to one another in the fear of God. Wives, submit to your own husbands, as to the Lord. For the husband is head of the wife, as also Christ is head of the church; and He is the Savior of the body. So husbands ought to love their own wives as their own bodies; he who loves his wife loves himself. For no one ever hated his own flesh, but nourishes and cherishes it, just as the Lord does the church. For this reason a man shall leave his father and mother and be joined to his wife, and the two shall become one flesh. Nevertheless let each one of you in particular so love his own wife as himself, and let the wife see that she respects her husband.

I Peter 3:7
Husbands, likewise, dwell with them with understanding, giving honor to the wife, as to the weaker vessel, and as being heirs together of the grace of life, that your prayers may not be hindered.

RENEWAL THOUGHT
There is something that happens in the heart and soul of a woman when her husband is spiritually growing.

JOY

As you put your trust in God you will rejoice. You do not need to wonder, be in fear, worry over whether or not you are going to make it. God is your defender. He is your guard.

Too often we try to take on the world all by ourselves. We say, "Bless God, I'm tough!" Well, why do something you do not have to? God's Word says to rejoice, recognizing that as we rejoice, we bring in the power and protection of God.

The Fulfilled Woman, Wendy Treat

Nehemiah 8:10
Then he said to them, "Go your way, eat the fat, drink the sweet, and send portions to those for whom nothing is prepared; for this day is holy to our LORD. Do not sorrow, for the joy of the LORD is your strength."

Psalm 16:11
You will show me the path of life; in Your presence is fullness of joy; at Your right hand are pleasures forevermore.

Psalm 35:27
Let them shout for joy and be glad, who favor my righteous cause; and let them say continually, "Let the LORD be magnified, who has pleasure in the prosperity of His servant."

John 15:11
These things I have spoken to you, that My joy may remain in you, and that your joy may be full.

Romans 14:17
For the kingdom of God is not eating and drinking, but righteousness and peace and joy in the Holy Spirit.

Galatians 5:22
But the fruit of the Spirit is love, joy, peace, longsuffering, kindness, goodness, faithfulness.

Philippians 4:4
Rejoice in the Lord always. Again I will say, rejoice!

James 1:2-4
My brethren, count it all joy when you fall into various trials, knowing that the testing of your faith produces patience. But let patience have its perfect work, that you may be perfect and complete, lacking nothing.

RENEWAL THOUGHT
If I choose to rejoice in the midst of the test then I am one step closer to victory in that trial.

KNOWLEDGE

Some of us have not developed our minds. The brain is the most under-developed muscle in the human race. Pump it up, man, that muscle between your ears. Don't walk in the futility of your mind. Don't turn your brain off. Some folks never think, never study, never question, never learn. They just go through the church motions. Get your mind right with God, not only your heart but your mind! Get plugged in to the knowledge and the understanding and the wisdom of God.

If we want to be this new creature in Christ, we've got to renew our mind with the knowledge of God. We've got to put on the new man, begin to think the thoughts of God and walk in His ways. That's when we have knowledge and understanding and wisdom.

The Benefits of Godly Wisdom, Casey Treat

Hosea 4:6
My people are destroyed for lack of knowledge. Because you have rejected knowledge, I also will reject you from being priest for Me; because you have forgotten the law of your God, I also will forget your children.

Romans 8:28
And we know that all things work together for good to those who love God, to those who are the called according to His purpose.

I Corinthians 13:9,12

For we know in part and we prophesy in part. For now we see in a mirror, dimly, but then face to face. Now I know in part, but then I shall know just as I also am known.

Ephesians 1:16-18

Do not cease to give thanks for you, making mention of you in my prayers: that the God of our Lord Jesus Christ, the Father of glory, may give to you the spirit of wisdom and revelation in the knowledge of Him, the eyes of your understanding being enlightened; that you may know what is the hope of His calling, what are the riches of the glory of His inheritance in the saints.

Philippians 3:10

That I may know Him and the power of His resurrection, and the fellowship of His sufferings, being conformed to His death.

I John 2:3

Now by this we know that we know Him, if we keep His commandments.

I John 5:14-15

Now this is the confidence that we have in Him, that if we ask anything according to His will, He hears us. And if we know that He hears us, whatever we ask, we know that we have the petitions that we have asked of Him.

RENEWAL THOUGHT

You must plan to feed your mind, otherwise your mind is going to atrophy.

LONELINESS

What I give out to others is what will be given back to me. The amount I give out is the amount which is given back to me. If you want more love in your life, how do you get it? Get out and start loving folks. Find someone to love. Find someone you haven't met and love them. Build them up, encourage them, and say something good. You say, "Oh, but, I'm kind of shy." There's no fear in love. Perfect love casts out fear and when that fear tries to stop you, just act in love and bulldoze it right over.

Casey Treat

Proverbs 18:24
A man who has friends must himself be friendly, but there is a friend who sticks closer than a brother.

Acts 2:42
And they continued steadfastly in the apostles' doctrine and fellowship, in the breaking of bread, and in prayers.

Hebrews 10:25
Not forsaking the assembling of ourselves together, as is the manner of some, but exhorting one another, and so much the more as you see the Day approaching.

Hebrews 13:5
Let your conduct be without covetousness; be con-

tent with such things as you have. For He Himself has said, "I will never leave you nor forsake you."

RENEWAL THOUGHT

Start looking for ways to help others. While you are teaching them and praying for them and loving them and building them up, your own doubts, fears and depressions will disappear.

LOVE

Christian love is not an impulse from a feeling. It doesn't always run with natural inclinations. It seeks the welfare of all. It is only known by the actions that it prompts.

If there is no action, there is no love. Love is only known by the actions that it prompts. When you open your mouth and spew out evil words to a person, that is hating them. Love opens its mouth and speaks good words.

Casey Treat

Matthew 5:44

But I say to you, love your enemies, bless those who curse you, do good to those who hate you, and pray for those who spitefully use you and persecute you.

Matthew 22:36-40

"Teacher, which is the great commandment in the law?" Jesus said to him, " 'You shall love the Lord your God with all your heart, with all your soul, and with all your mind.' This is the first and great commandment. And the second is like it: 'You shall love your neighbor as yourself.' On these two commandments hang all the Law and the Prophets."

John 3:16

For God so loved the world that He gave His only begotten Son, that whoever believes in Him should not perish but have everlasting life.

John 15:12-14

This is My commandment, that you love one another as I have loved you. Greater love has no one than this, than to lay down one's life for his friends. You are My friends if you do whatever I command you.

Romans 5:5

Now hope does not disappoint, because the love of God has been poured out in our hearts by the Holy Spirit who was given to us.

Romans 8:37-39

Yet in all these things we are more than conquerors through Him who loved us. For I am persuaded that neither death nor life, nor angels nor principalities nor powers, nor things present nor things to come, nor height nor depth, nor any other created thing, shall be able to separate us from the love of God which is in Christ Jesus our Lord.

I Corinthians 13:1-8

Though I speak with the tongues of men and of angels, but have not love, I have become sounding brass or a clanging cymbal. And though I have the gift of prophecy, and understand all mysteries and all knowledge, and though I have all faith, so that I could remove mountains, but have not love, I am nothing. And though I bestow all my goods to feed the poor, and though I give my body to be burned, but have not love, it profits me nothing. Love suffers long and is kind; love does not envy; love does not parade itself, is not puffed up; does not behave rudely, does not seek its own, is not provoked, thinks no evil; does not rejoice in iniquity, but rejoices in the truth; bears all things, believes all things, hopes all things, endures all things. Love never fails. But whether there are prophecies, they will fail; whether there are tongues, they will cease; whether there is knowledge, it will vanish away.

I John 4:7,8
Beloved, let us love one another, for love is of God; and everyone who loves is born of God and knows God. He who does not love does not know God, for God is love.

I John 4:18-20
There is no fear in love; but perfect love casts out fear, because fear involves torment. But he who fears has not been made perfect in love. We love Him because He first loved us. If someone says, "I love God," and hates his brother, he is a liar; for he who does not love his brother whom he has seen, how can he love God whom he has not seen?

RENEWAL THOUGHT
Love is the way that you act toward people at all times.

MARRIAGE

Marriage can be the most wonderful, intimate relationship possible between two people. Or it can be the worst nightmare you can imagine. You can have a trusting, open, happy, fun relationship, or you can have a hurting, demoralizing and very painful relationship. And, of course, since the devil recognizes that the marriage relationship can bring such good or evil into a person's life, he is going to really go after that relationship. He wants to bring you down into the depths of despair. So, in a sense he's really going after you as an individual. He wants to destroy you personally, and since your marriage is a huge part of you, he also wants to destroy your marriage.

God's plan was not men against women, women against men. Adam was created, and he wanted and needed a woman. God agreed and made Adam a helpmate. God took woman from the side of man. She was to be his helpmate. She was created as his partner; to have fun with, to rule and reign together, to grow and mature and do the things of God on this earth. He so clearly teaches us through the New Testament that there is neither male nor female, there is neither bond nor free, that we are one in Christ.

<u>Battle of the Sexes</u>, Wendy Treat

Genesis 2:24
Therefore a man shall leave his father and mother and be joined to his wife, and they shall become one flesh.

Proverbs 18:22
He who finds a wife finds a good thing, and obtains favor from the LORD.

Mark 10:2-9
The Pharisees came and asked Him, "Is it lawful for a man to divorce his wife?" testing Him. And He answered and said to them, "What did Moses command you?" They said, "Moses permitted a man to write a certificate of divorce, and to dismiss her." And Jesus answered and said to them, "Because of the hardness of your heart he wrote you this precept. But from the beginning of the creation, God 'made them male and female. For this reason a man shall leave his father and mother and be joined to his wife, and the two shall become one flesh'; so then they are no longer two, but one flesh. Therefore what God has joined together, let not man separate."

I Timothy 3:12
Let deacons be the husbands of one wife, ruling their children and their own houses well.

I Timothy 5:14
Therefore I desire that the younger widows marry, bear children, manage the house, give no opportunity to the adversary to speak reproachfully.

Hebrews 13:4
Marriage is honorable among all, and the bed undefiled; but fornicators and adulterers God will judge.

RENEWAL THOUGHT

Good marriages don't just happen! You have to decide to never quit growing, learning, loving and giving to your mate.

MEDITATION

Though most people don't realize, we all meditate day and night. Meditation is simply thinking about something. The Hebrew word is to think on, ponder, mutter to oneself, or picture in the mind. It is impossible to not think about anything, so we meditate all our waking hours. The question is, what are you meditating on? Is your mind focused on the things of God, and His way of dealing with the issues you are facing? Or are you thinking on thoughts of anger, frustration, bitterness, anxiety, and so forth? God says the things you meditate on are deciding whether you prosper and have good success, or struggle through life just trying to make a living.

<u>Renewing the Mind</u>, Casey Treat

Joshua 1:8
This Book of the Law shall not depart from your mouth, but you shall meditate in it day and night, that you may observe to do according to all that is written in it. For then you will make your way prosperous, and then you will have good success.

Psalm 1:1-3
Blessed is the man who walks not in the counsel of the ungodly, nor stands in the path of sinners, nor sits in the seat of the scornful; but his delight is in the law of the LORD, and in His law he meditates day and night. He shall be like a tree planted by the rivers of water, that brings forth its fruit in its sea-

son, whose leaf also shall not wither; and whatever he does shall prosper.

Psalm 19:14
Let the words of my mouth and the meditation of my heart be acceptable in Your sight, O LORD, my strength and my Redeemer.

Psalm 63:5-6
My soul shall be satisfied as with marrow and fatness, and my mouth shall praise You with joyful lips. When I remember You on my bed, I meditate on You in the night watches.

Psalm 119:99
I have more understanding than all my teachers, for Your testimonies are my meditation.

Philippians 4:8
Finally, brethren, whatever things are true, whatever things are noble, whatever things are just, whatever things are pure, whatever things are lovely, whatever things are of good report, if there is any virtue and if there is anything praiseworthy— meditate on these things.

I Timothy 4:15
Meditate on these things; give yourself entirely to them, that your progress may be evident to all.

RENEWAL THOUGHT
As you refocus your mind, you take a new picture of your future.

MONEY

Though the world is motivated by money and every minute people sell their souls, their marriages, their bodies, and their lives for money, as Christians we must live a higher level of life.

We all pray for God to bless our jobs or efforts, so we must believe that He wants us to prosper in some way. We know God does not cause or desire the people of this world to die of starvation or sickness. What does God mean when He says, "He will give you the power to get wealth" in Deuteronomy 8:18, and what does "prosper and have good success," which He promised in Joshua 1:8, really mean?

I'm sure Matthew 6:33 is a verse of scripture that gives balance to what our attitude about money should be. Seeking the kingdom of God and His righteousness is to be the first priority of the Christian life. The marriage, family, house, career, position, vacation, boat, cabin. . . are all to be somewhere down the list of priorities. By saying "first" Jesus is letting us know that we can and will seek other things. He didn't say "seek only," however, we must guard our hearts or we soon find ourselves seeking everything but the Kingdom of God.

<u>Errors of the Prosperity Gospel</u>, Casey Treat

Deuteronomy 8:18
And you shall remember the LORD your God, for it is He who gives you power to get wealth, that He may establish His covenant which He swore to your fathers, as it is this day.

139

Deuteronomy 28:2-6,8

And all these blessings shall come upon you and overtake you, because you obey the voice of the LORD your God: Blessed shall you be in the city, and blessed shall you be in the country. Blessed shall be the fruit of your body, the produce of your ground and the increase of your herds, the increase of your cattle and the offspring of your flocks. Blessed shall be your basket and your kneading bowl. Blessed shall you be when you come in, and blessed shall you be when you go out. The LORD will command the blessing on you in your storehouses and in all to which you set your hand, and He will bless you in the land which the LORD your God is giving you.

Psalm 1:1-3

Blessed is the man who walks not in the counsel of the ungodly, nor stands in the path of sinners, nor sits in the seat of the scornful; but his delight is in the law of the LORD, and in His law he meditates day and night. He shall be like a tree planted by the rivers of water, that brings forth its fruit in its season, whose leaf also shall not wither; and whatever he does shall prosper.

Malachi 3:8-11

"Will a man rob God? Yet you have robbed Me! But you say, 'In what way have we robbed You?' In tithes and offerings. You are cursed with a curse, for you have robbed Me, even this whole nation. Bring all the tithes into the storehouse, that there may be food in My house, and try Me now in this," says the LORD of hosts, "If I will not open for you the windows of heaven and pour out for you such blessing that there will not be room enough to receive it. And I will rebuke the devourer for your sakes, so that he will not destroy the fruit of your ground, nor shall the vine fail to bear fruit for you in the field," says the LORD of hosts.

Matthew 6:24-34

No one can serve two masters; for either he will hate the one and love the other, or else he will be loyal to the one and despise the other. You cannot serve God and mammon. Therefore I say to you, do not worry about your life, what you will eat or what you will drink; nor about your body, what you will put on. Is not life more than food and the body more than clothing? Look at the birds of the air, for they neither sow nor reap nor gather into barns; yet your heavenly Father feeds them. Are you not of more value than they? Which of you by worrying can add one cubit to his stature? So why do you worry about clothing? Consider the lilies of the field, how they grow: they neither toil nor spin; and yet I say to you that even Solomon in all his glory was not arrayed like one of these. Now if God so clothes the grass of the field, which today is, and tomorrow is thrown into the oven, will He not much more clothe you, O you of little faith? Therefore do not worry, saying, "What shall we eat?" or "What shall we drink?" or "What shall we wear?" For after all these things the Gentiles seek. For your heavenly Father knows that you need all these things. But seek first the kingdom of God and His righteousness, and all these things shall be added to you. Therefore do not worry about tomorrow, for tomorrow will worry about its own things. Sufficient for the day is its own trouble.

Mark 10:17-30

Now as He was going out on the road, one came running, knelt before Him, and asked Him, "Good Teacher, what shall I do that I may inherit eternal life?" So Jesus said to him, "Why do you call Me good? No one is good but One, that is, God. You know the commandments: 'Do not commit adultery,' 'Do not murder,' 'Do not steal,' 'Do not bear false witness,' 'Do not defraud,' 'Honor your father and your mother.'" And he answered and said to Him, "Teacher, all these I have observed from my youth." Then Jesus, looking at him, loved him, and said to him, "One thing you lack: Go your way, sell whatever you have and give to the poor, and you will have treasure in heaven; and come, take up the cross, and follow Me." But he was sad at this word, and went away sorrowful, for he had great possessions. Then Jesus looked around and said to His disciples, "How hard it is for those who have riches to enter the kingdom of God!" And the disciples were astonished at His words. But Jesus answered again and said to them, "Children, how hard it is for those who trust in riches to enter the kingdom of God! It is easier for a camel to go through the eye of a needle than for a rich man to enter the kingdom of God." And they were greatly astonished, saying among themselves, "Who then can be saved?" But Jesus looked at them and said, "With men it is impossible, but not with God; for with

God all things are possible." Then Peter began to say to Him, "See, we have left all and followed You." So Jesus answered and said, "Assuredly, I say to you, there is no one who has left house or brothers or sisters or father or mother or wife or children or lands, for My sake and the gospel's, who shall not receive a hundredfold now in this time— houses and brothers and sisters and mothers and children and lands, with persecutions— and in the age to come, eternal life.

II Corinthians 8:9

For you know the grace of our Lord Jesus Christ, that though He was rich, yet for your sakes He became poor, that you through His poverty might become rich.

II Corinthians 9:6-8

But this I say: He who sows sparingly will also reap sparingly, and he who sows bountifully will also reap bountifully. So let each one give as he purposes in his heart, not grudgingly or of necessity; for God loves a cheerful giver. And God is able to make all grace abound toward you, that you, always having all sufficiency in all things, may have an abundance for every good work.

Galatians 3:13-14

Christ has redeemed us from the curse of the law, having become a curse for us (for it is written, "Cursed is everyone who hangs on a tree"), that the blessing of Abraham might come upon the Gentiles in Christ Jesus, that we might receive the promise of the Spirit through faith.

Philippians 4:19
And my God shall supply all your need according to His riches in glory by Christ Jesus.

I Timothy 6:6-10
Now godliness with contentment is great gain. For we brought nothing into this world, and it is certain we can carry nothing out. And having food and clothing, with these we shall be content. But those who desire to be rich fall into temptation and a snare, and into many foolish and harmful lusts which drown men in destruction and perdition. For the love of money is a root of all kinds of evil, for which some have strayed from the faith in their greediness, and pierced themselves through with many sorrows.

I Timothy 6:17-19
Command those who are rich in this present age not to be haughty, nor to trust in uncertain riches but in the living God, who gives us richly all things to enjoy. Let them do good, that they be rich in good works, ready to give, willing to share, storing up for themselves a good foundation for the time to come, that they may lay hold on eternal life.

III John 2
Beloved, I pray that you may prosper in all things and be in health, just as your soul prospers.

RENEWAL THOUGHT
Put your money in Heaven's bank where it is secure, and you can count on a return on your investment.

OBEDIENCE

The fear of the Lord! We need more of that in our society. Today people stand before God and mock Him and say, " I love God. . ." But then without fear, without any shame, without any disgrace they openly disobey. They have no fear of God.

You can't lie to God, jive God, sit in church and lift your hands and say, "You are Lord," and go out and live like you feel like living and expect to have the knowledge, understanding and wisdom of God. You just can't. If you try you're playing the fool.

I know folks who say, "I tithe because I'm afraid of what would happen if I didn't." I don't think that's the highest level of motivation, but those who act out of the fear of the Lord are still doing better than those who don't tithe. There is no fear of God in the hearts of those who don't tithe.

Some of you were raised in homes that had a little of that "old time religion" - that legalistic mindset. Even though you didn't always like some of the rules, you had a fear of God. Maybe you got mad and bitter at some of the religious rules; maybe you even did your own thing. But that fear of God stayed with you.

The beginning of all knowledge, the beginning of all understanding, the beginning of all wisdom is an awesome respect for the Lord which results in submission and surrender to God.

<u>The Benefits of Godly Wisdom</u>, Casey Treat

145

I Samuel 15:22-23
Then Samuel said: "Has the LORD as great delight in burnt offerings and sacrifices, as in obeying the voice of the LORD? Behold, to obey is better than sacrifice, and to heed than the fat of rams. For rebellion is as the sin of witchcraft, and stubbornness is as iniquity and idolatry. Because you have rejected the word of the LORD, he also has rejected you from being king."

II Kings 5:13,14
And his servants came near and spoke to him, and said, "My father, if the prophet had told you to do something great, would you not have done it? How much more then, when he says to you, 'Wash, and be clean'?" So he went down and dipped seven times in the Jordan, according to the saying of the man of God; and his flesh was restored like the flesh of a little child, and he was clean.

Isaiah 1:19
If you are willing and obedient, you shall eat the good of the land;

Matthew 7:21-23
Not everyone who says to Me, "Lord, Lord," shall enter the kingdom of heaven, but he who does the will of My Father in heaven. Many will say to Me in that day, "Lord, Lord, have we not prophesied in Your name, cast out demons in Your name, and done many wonders in Your name?" And then I will declare to them, "I never knew you; depart from Me, you who practice lawlessness!"

Luke 6:46-49

But why do you call Me "Lord, Lord," and do not do the things which I say? Whoever comes to Me, and hears My sayings and does them, I will show you whom he is like: He is like a man building a house, who dug deep and laid the foundation on the rock. And when the flood arose, the stream beat vehemently against that house, and could not shake it, for it was founded on the rock. But he who heard and did nothing is like a man who built a house on the earth without a foundation, against which the stream beat vehemently; and immediately it fell. And the ruin of that house was great.

Ephesians 6:1

Children, obey your parents in the Lord, for this is right.

James 2:14,17,26

What does it profit, my brethren, if someone says he has faith but does not have works? Can faith save him? Thus also faith by itself, if it does not have works, is dead. For as the body without the spirit is dead, so faith without works is dead also.

RENEWAL THOUGHT

We can capture every thought, and bring it to the obedience of the Word of God.

OPPRESSION

If you were in a war and you were resisting the attack of the enemy, you'd have to be ready to resist airplanes, missiles, submarines, boats, troops, germ warfare, and propaganda. You'd have to be able to resist that enemy in many different ways. If the enemy knew that your resistance was strong for airplanes but weak for boats, he'd float you a boat. The devil comes at people in a lot of different ways and many Christians are not prepared to handle them. We haven't put up our guard. We have not realized that we have an enemy and he is on the attack. Because of that we never get strong, confident, and powerful in God. We always stay just bumping along.

It's possible to quench every fiery dart that Satan throws your way. What are the fiery darts? They are the thoughts, the negative messages, the evil teaching, that Satan throws at us all the time. You can resist those things if you'll keep the shield of faith up.

Casey Treat

Joshua 1:9
Have I not commanded you? Be strong and of good courage; do not be afraid, nor be dismayed, for the LORD your God is with you wherever you go.

Luke 13:11-16
And behold, there was a woman who had a spirit of infirmity eighteen years, and was bent over and

could in no way raise herself up. But when Jesus saw her, He called her to Him and said to her, "Woman, you are loosed from your infirmity." And He laid His hands on her, and immediately she was made straight, and glorified God. But the ruler of the synagogue answered with indignation, because Jesus had healed on the Sabbath; and he said to the crowd, "There are six days on which men ought to work; therefore come and be healed on them, and not on the Sabbath day." The Lord then answered him and said, "Hypocrite! Does not each one of you on the Sabbath loose his ox or donkey from the stall, and lead it away to water it? So ought not this woman, being a daughter of Abraham, whom Satan has bound— think of it— for eighteen years, be loosed from this bond on the Sabbath?"

Acts 10:38
How God anointed Jesus of Nazareth with the Holy Spirit and with power, who went about doing good and healing all who were oppressed by the devil, for God was with Him.

II Corinthians 10:4-5
For the weapons of our warfare are not carnal but mighty in God for pulling down strongholds, casting down arguments and every high thing that exalts itself against the knowledge of God, bringing every thought into captivity to the obedience of Christ.

Ephesians 6:10-16
Finally, my brethren, be strong in the Lord and in

the power of His might. Put on the whole armor of God, that you may be able to stand against the wiles of the devil. For we do not wrestle against flesh and blood, but against principalities, against powers, against the rulers of the darkness of this age, against spiritual hosts of wickedness in the heavenly places. Therefore take up the whole armor of God, that you may be able to withstand in the evil day, and having done all, to stand. Stand therefore, having girded your waist with truth, having put on the breastplate of righteousness, and having shod your feet with the preparation of the gospel of peace; above all, taking the shield of faith with which you will be able to quench all the fiery darts of the wicked one.

James 4:7
Therefore submit to God. Resist the devil and he will flee from you.

RENEWAL THOUGHT
The devil can bring evil circumstances, but we decide how we will respond to those circumstances.

Parenting

Before making the decision to have children we knew we had some worldly thinking we needed to change. We had been told by people around us that children would mess up our lifestyle, slow us down and take a lot of fun out of life. We believed that when we had children there would be many things we couldn't do anymore, and people confirmed our thinking all the time by their negative attitudes. Therefore, we were reluctant to have children for several years.

We had been married for over five years before we began to renew our minds about having children. We saw that many things the world said were perverted. If we would think the opposite of what the world said, we would get a pretty clear picture of what the truth was.

We saw the reality of the blessing from God that children are. We also saw that we could handle the responsibility. We realized that the things we don't know about are known to God and He is going to help us. We realized if God has helped us to succeed in so many other areas, even though we didn't know everything about them, God could help us to succeed in having children and being parents. When we asked God to help us and give us wisdom in the areas we didn't know about, the fear and worry about raising children left.

<u>Positive Childbirth</u>, Casey and Wendy Treat

Deuteronomy 4:9
Only take heed to yourself, and diligently keep your-

151

self, lest you forget the things your eyes have seen, and lest they depart from your heart all the days of your life. And teach them to your children and your grandchildren.

Deuteronomy 6:7
You shall teach them diligently to your children, and shall talk of them when you sit in your house, when you walk by the way, when you lie down, and when you rise up.

II Chronicles 26:4
And he did what was right in the sight of the LORD, according to all that his father Amaziah had done.

Proverbs 13:24
He who spares his rod hates his son, but he who loves him disciplines him promptly.

Proverbs 19:18
Chasten your son while there is hope, and do not set your heart on his destruction.

Proverbs 22:6
Train up a child in the way he should go, and when he is old he will not depart from it.

Proverbs 23:13
Do not withhold correction from a child, for if you beat him with a rod, he will not die.

Ephesians 6:1-4
Children, obey your parents in the Lord, for this is right. "Honor your father and mother," which is

the first commandment with promise: "that it may
be well with you and you may live long on the
earth." And you, fathers, do not provoke your children to wrath, but bring them up in the training and
admonition of the Lord.

II Timothy 1:5
When I call to remembrance the genuine faith that
is in you, which dwelt first in your grandmother
Lois and your mother Eunice, and I am persuaded
is in you also.

Renewal Thought

*Once you have your own children, you appreciate
your parents so much more.*

PATIENCE

The trying of our faith is going to produce patience. That's not easy but that's reality. Sometimes the Lord just has to leave us in the oven for awhile. And so God says to us, "There are some things that you're going to have to learn and it will take time. Your faith is going to be tested. But if you will stand and develop patience through this thing, you'll become a wiser and better person."

The Word says, "Count it all joy. . ." Know your faith is being tested and let that patience develop. If you rejoice, you stand even in the midst of the test and go on with what you know God told you to do. By the end of the test you are saying, "Yeah, I didn't necessarily enjoy it, but I'm better off." There is a strength and security and confidence that you can't have unless you go through the test.

<u>The Benefits of Godly Wisdom</u>, Casey Treat

Psalm 37:7
Rest in the LORD, and wait patiently for Him; do not fret because of him who prospers in his way, because of the man who brings wicked schemes to pass.

Psalm 40:1-3
I waited patiently for the LORD; and He inclined to me, and heard my cry. He also brought me up out of a horrible pit, out of the miry clay, and set my feet upon a rock, and established my steps. He

has put a new song in my mouth— praise to our God; many will see it and fear, and will trust in the LORD.

Hebrews 6:12,15
That you do not become sluggish, but imitate those who through faith and patience inherit the promises. And so, after he had patiently endured, he obtained the promise.

Hebrews 10:35-36
Therefore do not cast away your confidence, which has great reward. For you have need of endurance, so that after you have done the will of God, you may receive the promise.

James 1:2-4
My brethren, count it all joy when you fall into various trials, knowing that the testing of your faith produces patience. But let patience have its perfect work, that you may be perfect and complete, lacking nothing.

RENEWAL THOUGHT
Nothing happens as quickly as we wish it would. Take the daily steps, don't give up, you will get there.

PEACE

Too often we get caught up in the cares of this life. Problems at the office, not enough money for all our needs, society is going down hill fast, we had another fight with our mate, we don't like who our kids are hanging around with, we're worried about the future. The list can go on and on. Unfortunately, the list does go on and on in many of your minds. That's why you must decide to be a person who lives at peace; with God, with yourself and with others.

In going for the very best, you must develop peace within yourself. Allow the peace of God to rule in your heart, not what the news says, or what another person does. You will never have peace in your life until you decide that you are in control of your own life. Then you can let the peace of God rule in your heart and mind.

The Fulfilled Woman, Wendy Treat

Numbers 6:26
The LORD lift up His countenance upon you, and give you peace.

Psalm 29:11
The LORD will give strength to His people; the LORD will bless His people with peace.

Luke 2:14
Glory to God in the highest, and on earth peace, goodwill toward men!

John 14:27
Peace I leave with you, My peace I give to you; not as the world gives do I give to you. Let not your heart be troubled, neither let it be afraid.

John 16:33
These things I have spoken to you, that in Me you may have peace. In the world you will have tribulation; but be of good cheer, I have overcome the world.

Romans 5:1
Therefore, having been justified by faith, we have peace with God through our Lord Jesus Christ.

Romans 14:17
For the kingdom of God is not eating and drinking, but righteousness and peace and joy in the Holy Spirit.

II Corinthians 13:11
Finally, brethren, farewell. Become complete. Be of good comfort, be of one mind, live in peace; and the God of love and peace will be with you.

Galatians 1:3
Grace to you and peace from God the Father and our Lord Jesus Christ.

Galatians 5:22
But the fruit of the Spirit is love, joy, peace, longsuffering, kindness, goodness, faithfulness.

Ephesians 2:14
For He Himself is our peace, who has made both one, and has broken down the middle wall of separation.

Philippians 4:6-7
Be anxious for nothing, but in everything by prayer and supplication, with thanksgiving, let your requests be made known to God; and the peace of God, which surpasses all understanding, will guard your hearts and minds through Christ Jesus.

Colossians 3:15
And let the peace of God rule in your hearts, to which also you were called in one body; and be thankful.

II Thessalonians 3:16
Now may the Lord of peace Himself give you peace always in every way. The Lord be with you all.

RENEWAL THOUGHT
Our focus in life is to share the gospel of peace.

PERSECUTION

Endure hardship! So many of us today shy away from hardship. If it's hard, it must not be the Lord! If it's hard, it can't be God's will. God is a God of war. He will not lead you into easiness, He will lead you into battle. The battle will be hard, but here's the exciting part: you will always win if you follow God!

Doing the will of God doesn't mean we go the easy way. We're fighting a battle and whether it's hard or not is not the issue. We are commanded to endure hardness as good soldiers, and to go into all the world and make disciples.

<u>Fighting for Excellence in Leadership</u>, Casey Treat

Matthew 5:11-12
Blessed are you when they revile and persecute you, and say all kinds of evil against you falsely for My sake. Rejoice and be exceedingly glad, for great is your reward in heaven, for so they persecuted the prophets who were before you.

Mark 4:16-17
These likewise are the ones sown on stony ground who, when they hear the word, immediately receive it with gladness; and they have no root in themselves, and so endure only for a time. Afterward, when tribulation or persecution arises for the word's sake, immediately they stumble.

John 15:20
Remember the word that I said to you, "A servant is not greater than his master." If they persecuted Me, they will also persecute you. If they kept My word, they will keep yours also.

Romans 8:35,37
Who shall separate us from the love of Christ? Shall tribulation, or distress, or persecution, or famine, or nakedness, or peril, or sword? Yet in all these things we are more than conquerors through Him who loved us.

Romans 12:14
Bless those who persecute you; bless and do not curse.

II Timothy 3:12
Yes, and all who desire to live godly in Christ Jesus will suffer persecution.

RENEWAL THOUGHT

The enemy wants to get rid of you! He attacks because you are using your faith. Keep using it, resist him, and win the battle!

PRAISE

Many times we have been watching TV and listening to negative news, so when we come to church we are worrying, or we may have been fighting with the kids. We come in from all different directions and plop down in the meeting place. Many times our minds are not on the Lord. As we begin to sing and minister unto the Lord in music, the anointing begins to flow through the church. We get in one accord and our mind gets centered on the Lord. We are able to receive from the Word and from the gifts of the Spirit.

<u>Setting Your Course</u>, Casey Treat

II Chronicles 5:13-14
Indeed it came to pass, when the trumpeters and singers were as one, to make one sound to be heard in praising and thanking the LORD, and when they lifted up their voice with the trumpets and cymbals and instruments of music, and praised the LORD, saying: "For He is good, for His mercy endures forever," that the house, the house of the LORD, was filled with a cloud, so that the priests could not continue ministering because of the cloud; for the glory of the LORD filled the house of God.

Psalm 28:2,7
Hear the voice of my supplications when I cry to You, when I lift up my hands toward Your holy sanctuary. The LORD is my strength and my shield; my heart trusted in Him, and I am helped; therefore

my heart greatly rejoices, and with my song I will praise Him.

Psalm 35:28
And my tongue shall speak of Your righteousness and of Your praise all the day long.

Psalm 47:1
Oh, clap your hands, all you peoples! Shout to God with the voice of triumph!

Psalm 51:15
O Lord, open my lips, and my mouth shall show forth Your praise.

Psalm 63:4
Thus I will bless You while I live; I will lift up my hands in Your name.

Psalm 100:4
Enter into His gates with thanksgiving, and into His courts with praise. Be thankful to Him, and bless His name.

Psalm 103:1-4
Bless the LORD, O my soul; and all that is within me, bless His holy name! Bless the LORD, O my soul, and forget not all His benefits: who forgives all your iniquities, who heals all your diseases, who redeems your life from destruction, who crowns you with lovingkindness and tender mercies.

Psalm 150
Praise the LORD! Praise God in His sanctuary; praise Him in His mighty firmament! Praise Him

for His mighty acts; praise Him according to His excellent greatness! Praise Him with the sound of the trumpet; praise Him with the lute and harp! Praise Him with the timbrel and dance; praise Him with stringed instruments and flutes! Praise Him with loud cymbals; praise Him with clashing cymbals! Let everything that has breath praise the LORD. Praise the LORD!

Luke 2:20
Then the shepherds returned, glorifying and praising God for all the things that they had heard and seen, as it was told them.

Acts 2:47
. . . praising God and having favor with all the people. And the Lord added to the church daily those who were being saved.

Ephesians 5:18-20
And do not be drunk with wine, in which is dissipation; but be filled with the Spirit, speaking to one another in psalms and hymns and spiritual songs, singing and making melody in your heart to the Lord, giving thanks always for all things to God the Father in the name of our Lord Jesus Christ.

I Timothy 2:8
I desire therefore that the men pray everywhere, lifting up holy hands, without wrath and doubting.

RENEWAL THOUGHT
God inhabits the praises of His people.

PRAYER

Praise God, what a terrific tool prayer is! If you are going to be an effective witness, and if you are going to be committed to ministering to the lost and helping people to receive the Holy Spirit, you need to understand the importance of prayer. If you are going to have the success God wants you to have, it has to be a major portion of your life.

<u>Won By One</u>, Wendy Treat

I Chronicles 16:11
Seek the LORD and His strength; seek His face evermore!

Isaiah 65:24
It shall come to pass that before they call, I will answer; and while they are still speaking, I will hear.

Jeremiah 29:13
And you will seek Me and find Me, when you search for Me with all your heart.

Psalm 65:2
O You who hear prayer, to You all flesh will come.

Matthew 7:7-11
Ask, and it will be given to you; seek, and you will find; knock, and it will be opened to you. For everyone who asks receives, and he who seeks finds, and to him who knocks it will be opened. Or what man is there among you who, if his son asks for bread, will give him a stone? Or if he asks for a fish, will he give him a serpent? If you then, being

evil, know how to give good gifts to your children, how much more will your Father who is in heaven give good things to those who ask Him!

Matthew 18:19
Again I say to you that if two of you agree on earth concerning anything that they ask, it will be done for them by My Father in heaven.

Matthew 21:21-22
So Jesus answered and said to them, "Assuredly, I say to you, if you have faith and do not doubt, you will not only do what was done to the fig tree, but also if you say to this mountain, 'Be removed and be cast into the sea,' it will be done. And whatever things you ask in prayer, believing, you will receive."

Mark 11:24
Therefore I say to you, whatever things you ask when you pray, believe that you receive them, and you will have them.

Luke 11:9
So I say to you, ask, and it will be given to you; seek, and you will find; knock, and it will be opened to you.

Luke 18:1
Then He spoke a parable to them, that men always ought to pray and not lose heart.

John 15:7
If you abide in Me, and My words abide in you,

you will ask what you desire, and it shall be done for you.

John 16:24
Until now you have asked nothing in My name. Ask, and you will receive, that your joy may be full.

Romans 8:26-27
Likewise the Spirit also helps in our weaknesses. For we do not know what we should pray for as we ought, but the Spirit Himself makes intercession for us with groanings which cannot be uttered. Now He who searches the hearts knows what the mind of the Spirit is, because He makes intercession for the saints according to the will of God.

I Corinthians 14:13-15
Therefore let him who speaks in a tongue pray that he may interpret. For if I pray in a tongue, my spirit prays, but my understanding is unfruitful. What is the conclusion then? I will pray with the spirit, and I will also pray with the understanding. I will sing with the spirit, and I will also sing with the understanding.

Ephesians 6:18
. . . praying always with all prayer and supplication in the Spirit, being watchful to this end with all perseverance and supplication for all the saints.

I Thessalonians 5:17
Pray without ceasing.

James 5:13
Is anyone among you suffering? Let him pray. Is anyone cheerful? Let him sing psalms.

James 5:16-17
Confess your trespasses to one another, and pray for one another, that you may be healed. The effective, fervent prayer of a righteous man avails much. Elijah was a man with a nature like ours, and he prayed earnestly that it would not rain; and it did not rain on the land for three years and six months.

I John 3:22
And whatever we ask we receive from Him, because we keep His commandments and do those things that are pleasing in His sight.

I John 5:14-15
Now this is the confidence that we have in Him, that if we ask anything according to His will, He hears us. And if we know that He hears us, whatever we ask, we know that we have the petitions that we have asked of Him.

Revelation 5:8
Now when He had taken the scroll, the four living creatures and the twenty-four elders fell down before the Lamb, each having a harp, and golden bowls full of incense, which are the prayers of the saints.

RENEWAL THOUGHT

There is no way for you to effectively minister under the anointing of the Holy Spirit without having built yourself up in prayer.

PROSPERITY

Prosperity is when we have enough for our own needs and desires as well as enough to give to others. You can apply that to any realm of life. Spiritual prosperity is when your spiritual needs are met and you have enough to help someone with their spiritual needs. Physical prosperity is when you are healthy and strong and can go over and help someone else become healthy and strong. Financial prosperity is when you have more than enough for your family and your desires and you can help someone else to prosper. When you can send finances to missionaries and meet their needs, pay their bills, that's prosperity. That doesn't necessarily mean you are a millionaire. It simply means you have more than enough.

<u>Setting Your Course</u>, Casey Treat

Deuteronomy 8:18
And you shall remember the LORD your God, for it is He who gives you power to get wealth, that He may establish His covenant which He swore to your fathers, as it is this day.

Deuteronomy 28:1-2
Now it shall come to pass, if you diligently obey the voice of the LORD your God, to observe carefully all His commandments which I command you today, that the LORD your God will set you high above all nations of the earth. And all these blessings shall come upon you and overtake you, because you obey the voice of the LORD your God.

Psalm 34:10
The young lions lack and suffer hunger; but those who seek the LORD shall not lack any good thing.

Psalm 85:12
Yes, the LORD will give what is good; and our land will yield its increase.

Psalm 91
He who dwells in the secret place of the Most High shall abide under the shadow of the Almighty. I will say of the LORD, "He is my refuge and my fortress; my God, in Him I will trust." Surely He shall deliver you from the snare of the fowler and from the perilous pestilence. He shall cover you with His feathers, and under His wings you shall take refuge; his truth shall be your shield and buckler. You shall not be afraid of the terror by night, nor of the arrow that flies by day, nor of the pestilence that walks in darkness, nor of the destruction that lays waste at noonday. A thousand may fall at your side, and ten thousand at your right hand; but it shall not come near you. Only with your eyes shall you look, and see the reward of the wicked. Because you have made the LORD, who is my refuge, even the Most High, your dwelling place, no evil shall befall you, nor shall any plague come near your dwelling; for He shall give His angels charge over you, to keep you in all your ways. In their hands they shall bear you up, lest you dash your foot against a stone. You shall tread upon the lion and the cobra, the young lion and the serpent you shall trample underfoot. "Because he has set his love upon Me, therefore I will deliver him; I will

set him on high, because he has known My name. He shall call upon Me, and I will answer him; I will be with him in trouble; I will deliver him and honor him. With long life I will satisfy him, and show him My salvation."

Isaiah 1:19
If you are willing and obedient, you shall eat the good of the land.

Malachi 3:8-11
"Will a man rob God? Yet you have robbed Me! But you say, 'In what way have we robbed You?' In tithes and offerings. You are cursed with a curse, for you have robbed Me, even this whole nation. Bring all the tithes into the storehouse, that there may be food in My house, and try Me now in this," says the LORD of hosts, "If I will not open for you the windows of heaven and pour out for you such blessing that there will not be room enough to receive it. And I will rebuke the devourer for your sakes, so that he will not destroy the fruit of your ground, nor shall the vine fail to bear fruit for you in the field," says the LORD of hosts.

Matthew 6:33
But seek first the kingdom of God and His righteousness, and all these things shall be added to you.

II Corinthians 9:6-8
But this I say: He who sows sparingly will also reap sparingly, and he who sows bountifully will also reap bountifully. So let each one give as he purposes in his heart, not grudgingly or of necessity;

for God loves a cheerful giver. And God is able to make all grace abound toward you, that you, always having all sufficiency in all things, may have an abundance for every good work.

Galatians 3:13-14
Christ has redeemed us from the curse of the law, having become a curse for us (for it is written, "Cursed is everyone who hangs on a tree"), that the blessing of Abraham might come upon the Gentiles in Christ Jesus, that we might receive the promise of the Spirit through faith.

Philippians 4:9
The things which you learned and received and heard and saw in me, these do, and the God of peace will be with you.

III John 2
Beloved, I pray that you may prosper in all things and be in health, just as your soul prospers.

RENEWAL THOUGHT
Your soul, mind, emotions, and will must prosper, before your life will prosper.

PROTECTION

We are made in God's likeness and His image, and as long as we walk with Him no one is going to overcome us. "Oh, Brother Treat, the communists infiltrated the United States." I feel sorry for them. If they start messing around with us they're going to get burned. They can't win against God.

God our Father stands in front of us. Those enemies that come against us are consumed and burned up at His presence. We just come through the affairs of life saying, "Thank You, Father." No worry and no fear.

Casey Treat

Deuteronomy 28:7
The LORD will cause your enemies who rise against you to be defeated before your face; they shall come out against you one way and flee before you seven ways.

Psalm 23
The LORD is my shepherd; I shall not want. He makes me to lie down in green pastures; he leads me beside the still waters. He restores my soul; he leads me in the paths of righteousness for His name's sake. Yea, though I walk through the valley of the shadow of death, I will fear no evil; for You are with me; your rod and Your staff, they comfort me. You prepare a table before me in the presence of my enemies; you anoint my head with oil; my cup runs over. Surely goodness and mercy shall follow

me all the days of my life; and I will dwell in the house of the LORD forever.

Psalm 91:1-13
He who dwells in the secret place of the Most High shall abide under the shadow of the Almighty. I will say of the LORD, "He is my refuge and my fortress; my God, in Him I will trust." Surely He shall deliver you from the snare of the fowler and from the perilous pestilence. He shall cover you with His feathers, and under His wings you shall take refuge; his truth shall be your shield and buckler. You shall not be afraid of the terror by night, nor of the arrow that flies by day, nor of the pestilence that walks in darkness, nor of the destruction that lays waste at noonday. A thousand may fall at your side, and ten thousand at your right hand; but it shall not come near you. Only with your eyes shall you look, and see the reward of the wicked. Because you have made the LORD, who is my refuge, even the Most High, your dwelling place, no evil shall befall you, nor shall any plague come near your dwelling; for He shall give His angels charge over you, to keep you in all your ways. In their hands they shall bear you up, lest you dash your foot against a stone. You shall tread upon the lion and the cobra, the young lion and the serpent you shall trample underfoot.

Proverbs 16:7
When a man's ways please the LORD, he makes even his enemies to be at peace with him.

Isaiah 59:19
So shall they fear the name of the LORD from the west, and His glory from the rising of the sun; when the enemy comes in like a flood, the Spirit of the LORD will lift up a standard against him.

Malachi 3:10-11
"Bring all the tithes into the storehouse, that there may be food in My house, and try Me now in this," says the LORD of hosts, "If I will not open for you the windows of heaven and pour out for you such blessing that there will not be room enough to receive it. And I will rebuke the devourer for your sakes, so that he will not destroy the fruit of your ground, nor shall the vine fail to bear fruit for you in the field," says the LORD of hosts.

Luke 10:19
Behold, I give you the authority to trample on serpents and scorpions, and over all the power of the enemy, and nothing shall by any means hurt you.

Ephesians 6:11-17
Put on the whole armor of God, that you may be able to stand against the wiles of the devil. For we do not wrestle against flesh and blood, but against principalities, against powers, against the rulers of the darkness of this age, against spiritual hosts of wickedness in the heavenly places. Therefore take up the whole armor of God, that you may be able to withstand in the evil day, and having done all, to stand. Stand therefore, having girded your waist with truth, having put on the breastplate of righ-

teousness, and having shod your feet with the preparation of the gospel of peace; above all, taking the shield of faith with which you will be able to quench all the fiery darts of the wicked one. And take the helmet of salvation, and the sword of the Spirit, which is the word of God.

James 4:7
Therefore submit to God. Resist the devil and he will flee from you.

RENEWAL THOUGHT
There isn't anyone or anything that's going to overcome God.

PROVISION

God has always shown Himself as a loving Father who provides for His children. He created a beautiful, abundant world for us to live in, not a desert wasteland. He provided riches, variety and wealth beyond man's ability to use. He promised a fruitful life. . . and through Jesus, abundant life. He is El Shaddai, the God Who is more than enough. When Jesus went fishing, He brought in "boat-sinking, net-breaking loads." When He fed the multitudes, He gave them twelve baskets more than enough.

God's Provision, Casey Treat

Psalm 34:10
The young lions lack and suffer hunger; but those who seek the LORD shall not lack any good thing.

Psalm 37:25
I have been young, and now am old; yet I have not seen the righteous forsaken, nor his descendants begging bread.

Matthew 6:31-33
Therefore do not worry, saying, "What shall we eat?" or "What shall we drink?" or "What shall we wear?" For after all these things the Gentiles seek. For your heavenly Father knows that you need all these things. But seek first the kingdom of God and His righteousness, and all these things shall be added to you.

Philippians 4:19
And my God shall supply all your need according
to His riches in glory by Christ Jesus.

RENEWAL THOUGHT

*It is God's nature and desire to meet the needs of
all mankind. He has a plan for you to be blessed.*

Rapture

Some believe when we leave the earth during the rapture, the sinners, those who are not born again, will see us leave as Jesus did. Unsaved husbands and wives will watch their mates leave. That would be the best altar call they could ever see. If that doesn't get them saved, they're pretty hard-hearted. Some believe that the sinners will see us rising out of our houses, rising out of our cars. If I had an airline service, I'd make sure not to put two Christians in the cockpit. If both of them get raptured, that plane is in trouble.

I really don't know if the world will see us leave or if we will just be gone. John said in Revelation 4, that immediately he was in the spirit. Once we do enter the spirit world, the natural world won't see us anymore. We're just gone in the twinkling of an eye. "Where'd they go?" And then they'll go about excusing why we disappeared. They'll have all kinds of theories and ideas of what happened to several million Christians who just vanished off the planet, but whether they see us go or whether we are just gone, it doesn't matter. The fact is we are going to end up before the throne of God.

<u>Setting Your Course</u>, Casey Treat

Luke 17:26-36
And as it was in the days of Noah, so it will be also in the days of the Son of Man: They ate, they drank, they married wives, they were given in marriage, until the day that Noah entered the ark, and the flood came and destroyed them all. Likewise as it was

also in the days of Lot: They ate, they drank, they bought, they sold, they planted, they built; but on the day that Lot went out of Sodom it rained fire and brimstone from heaven and destroyed them all. Even so will it be in the day when the Son of Man is revealed. In that day, he who is on the housetop, and his goods are in the house, let him not come down to take them away. And likewise the one who is in the field, let him not turn back. Remember Lot's wife. Whoever seeks to save his life will lose it, and whoever loses his life will preserve it. I tell you, in that night there will be two men in one bed: the one will be taken and the other will be left. Two women will be grinding together: the one will be taken and the other left. Two men will be in the field: the one will be taken and the other left.

I Corinthians 15:51-57
Behold, I tell you a mystery: We shall not all sleep, but we shall all be changed—in a moment, in the twinkling of an eye, at the last trumpet. For the trumpet will sound, and the dead will be raised incorruptible, and we shall be changed. For this corruptible must put on incorruption, and this mortal must put on immortality. So when this corruptible has put on incorruption, and this mortal has put on immortality, then shall be brought to pass the saying that is written: "Death is swallowed up in victory." "O Death, where is your sting? O Hades, where is your victory?" The sting of death is sin, and the strength of sin is the law. But thanks be to God, who gives us the victory through our Lord Jesus Christ.

I Thessalonians 4:16-18
For the Lord Himself will descend from heaven with a shout, with the voice of an archangel, and with the trumpet of God. And the dead in Christ will rise first. Then we who are alive and remain shall be caught up together with them in the clouds to meet the Lord in the air. And thus we shall always be with the Lord. Therefore comfort one another with these words.

RENEWAL THOUGHT

There are going to be a lot of people repenting, crying, and calling out to God when all the Christians have suddenly disappeared.

Rebellion

A rebel at heart will never lead anybody in the Church. To be a good leader, you have to be a good follower. Those who want to do their own thing will never lead anybody, but those who know how to follow will soon become leaders. You have to get in line behind someone else before others can get in line behind you! In the Kingdom of God, you cannot start your own thing.

Casey Treat

Numbers 14:9
Only do not rebel against the LORD, nor fear the people of the land, for they are our bread; their protection has departed from them, and the LORD is with us. Do not fear them.

I Samuel 15:23
For rebellion is as the sin of witchcraft, and stubbornness is as iniquity and idolatry. Because you have rejected the word of the LORD, he also has rejected you from being king.

Psalm 78:7-8
That they may set their hope in God, and not forget the works of God, but keep His commandments; and may not be like their fathers, a stubborn and rebellious generation, a generation that did not set its heart aright, and whose spirit was not faithful to God.

Isaiah 1:19-20
"If you are willing and obedient, you shall eat the good of the land; but if you refuse and rebel, you shall be devoured by the sword"; for the mouth of the LORD has spoken.

Isaiah 63:10
But they rebelled and grieved His Holy Spirit; so He turned Himself against them as an enemy, and He fought against them.

Ephesians 6:1
Children, obey your parents in the Lord, for this is right.

RENEWAL THOUGHT

When you reject God, you can't receive the help or the provisions of God.

Renewing The Mind

One of the first lessons I learned as I began to build a new life was that my spirit was separated from God's Spirit. I needed a relationship with the One who created me and destined me for a fulfilled life. I could not have a relationship with God, an eternal destiny with Him, or His power in my life on earth until I was changed spiritually.

To grow spiritually is an on-going process of renewing your mind to the Word of God, reprogramming your thoughts with the thoughts of God, exchanging the way you think in the natural mind to the way God says we should think.

<u>Renewing the Mind</u>, Casey Treat

Proverbs 9:8
Do not correct a scoffer, lest he hate you; rebuke a wise man, and he will love you.

Proverbs 10:17
He who keeps instruction is in the way of life, but he who refuses correction goes astray.

Proverbs 12:1
Whoever loves instruction loves knowledge, but he who hates correction is stupid.

Proverbs 12:15
The way of a fool is right in his own eyes, but he who heeds counsel is wise.

Proverbs 24:6
For by wise counsel you will wage your own war, and in a multitude of counselors there is safety.

Proverbs 29:1
He who is often rebuked, and hardens his neck, will suddenly be destroyed, and that without remedy.

Romans 12:1-2
I beseech you therefore, brethren, by the mercies of God, that you present your bodies a living sacrifice, holy, acceptable to God, which is your reasonable service. And do not be conformed to this world, but be transformed by the renewing of your mind, that you may prove what is that good and acceptable and perfect will of God.

II Corinthians 10:5
. . . casting down arguments and every high thing that exalts itself against the knowledge of God, bringing every thought into captivity to the obedience of Christ.

Ephesians 4:24-25
. . . and that you put on the new man which was created according to God, in true righteousness and holiness. Therefore, putting away lying, "Let each one of you speak truth with his neighbor," for we are members of one another.

Colossians 3:10-13
. . . and have put on the new man who is renewed in knowledge according to the image of Him who created him, where there is neither Greek nor Jew, cir-

cumcised nor uncircumcised, barbarian, Scythian, slave nor free, but Christ is all and in all. Therefore, as the elect of God, holy and beloved, put on tender mercies, kindness, humility, meekness, longsuffering; bearing with one another, and forgiving one another, if anyone has a complaint against another; even as Christ forgave you, so you also must do.

II Timothy 1:7
For God has not given us a spirit of fear, but of power and of love and of a sound mind.

RENEWAL THOUGHT
To the degree that your mind is renewed, you will begin to experience change, and you will enter into a renewed life.

RIGHTEOUSNESS

When we are transformed by the renewing of our minds, we enjoy righteousness (right relationship with God), and are free from guilt and condemnation.

When we are born again, we are made the righteousness of God; but most people never enjoy that. They don't enjoy the freedom and the right relationship that they have. They're not free from guilt and condemnation. They aren't transformed; so they never put on the new man, which is renewed in knowledge after the image of Him that created them, in righteousness and true holiness.

Casey Treat

Psalm 34:15
The eyes of the LORD are on the righteous, and His ears are open to their cry.

Psalm 37:25
I have been young, and now am old; yet I have not seen the righteous forsaken, nor his descendants begging bread.

Psalm 92:12
The righteous shall flourish like a palm tree, he shall grow like a cedar in Lebanon.

Proverbs 15:19
The way of the lazy man is like a hedge of thorns, but the way of the upright is a highway.

Isaiah 3:10
Say to the righteous that it shall be well with them, for they shall eat the fruit of their doings.

Romans 5:17
For if by the one man's offense death reigned through the one, much more those who receive abundance of grace and of the gift of righteousness will reign in life through the One, Jesus Christ.

II Corinthians 5:20
Now then, we are ambassadors for Christ, as though God were pleading through us: we implore you on Christ's behalf, be reconciled to God.

Ephesians 6:14
Stand therefore, having girded your waist with truth, having put on the breastplate of righteousness.

Philippians 1:11
. . . being filled with the fruits of righteousness which are by Jesus Christ, to the glory and praise of God.

I Timothy 6:11
But you, O man of God, flee these things and pursue righteousness, godliness, faith, love, patience, gentleness.

RENEWAL THOUGHT
You're just as righteous today as you ever will be.

SALVATION

God so loved all people that He sent Jesus to save us from spiritual death. Spiritual death would be a tragedy if there was not a remedy, but He gave us salvation. He gave us a Saviour. What's His name? Jesus. The reason Jesus is our King and our Lord and the One we serve is because He saved us from that spiritual death. Whoever believes in Jesus won't die; they'll have everlasting life. Whoever believes in Jesus will be set free from the spiritual death that all mankind is subject to. We are born again. We become new people with new life, and we'll share that life for eternity with the Father.

Setting Your Course, Casey Treat

John 3:3-7,16-18
Jesus answered and said to him, "Most assuredly, I say to you, unless one is born again, he cannot see the kingdom of God." Nicodemus said to Him, "How can a man be born when he is old? Can he enter a second time into his mother's womb and be born?" Jesus answered, "Most assuredly, I say to you, unless one is born of water and the Spirit, he cannot enter the kingdom of God. That which is born of the flesh is flesh, and that which is born of the Spirit is spirit. Do not marvel that I said to you, 'You must be born again.' For God so loved the world that He gave His only begotten Son, that whoever believes in Him should not perish but have everlasting life. For God did not send His Son into the world to condemn the world, but that the world through Him might be saved. He who believes in

Him is not condemned; but he who does not believe is condemned already, because he has not believed in the name of the only begotten Son of God.

John 10:9
I am the door. If anyone enters by Me, he will be
saved, and will go in and out and find pasture.

Acts 2:21
And it shall come to pass that whoever calls on the
name of the Lord shall be saved.

Acts 4:12
Nor is there salvation in any other, for there is no
other name under heaven given among men by
which we must be saved.

Romans 5:18
Therefore, as through one man's offense judgment
came to all men, resulting in condemnation, even
so through one Man's righteous act the free gift
came to all men, resulting in justification of life.

Romans 6:23
For the wages of sin is death, but the gift of God is
eternal life in Christ Jesus our Lord.

Romans 10:9-10,13
. . . that if you confess with your mouth the Lord
Jesus and believe in your heart that God has raised
Him from the dead, you will be saved. For with the
heart one believes unto righteousness, and with the
mouth confession is made unto salvation. For "whoever calls on the name of the Lord shall be saved."

Ephesians 2:8
For by grace you have been saved through faith, and that not of yourselves; it is the gift of God.

I Timothy 2:4
. . . who desires all men to be saved and to come to the knowledge of the truth.

II Peter 3:9
The Lord is not slack concerning His promise, as some count slackness, but is longsuffering toward us, not willing that any should perish but that all should come to repentance.

Renewal Thought

Salvation is a gift from God, and all we do is receive it by faith in Jesus Christ.

SATAN

If Jesus is real in your life then you must also recognize the reality of your enemy. If it took the death of Christ to defeat him, it's going to take some dedication from you to complete that defeat and keep the devil from controlling your life. Jesus has stripped him of his authority, but just like any common criminal, thief, or murderer, he'll do whatever you let him get away with. He can't take your salvation but he can make you a non-effective Christian. The devil doesn't really care if you're saved or not as long as you don't go spreading salvation around. He wants to defeat you in any way that he can.

<u>Fighting For Excellence In Leadership</u>, Casey Treat

Genesis 3:14-15
So the LORD God said to the serpent: "Because you have done this, you are cursed more than all cattle, and more than every beast of the field; on your belly you shall go, and you shall eat dust all the days of your life. And I will put enmity between you and the woman, and between your seed and her Seed; he shall bruise your head, and you shall bruise His heel."

Isaiah 14:12-15
How you are fallen from heaven, O Lucifer, son of the morning! How you are cut down to the ground, you who weakened the nations! For you have said in your heart: "I will ascend into heaven, I will exalt my throne above the stars of God; I will also sit

on the mount of the congregation on the farthest sides of the north; I will ascend above the heights of the clouds, I will be like the Most High." Yet you shall be brought down to Sheol, to the lowest depths of the Pit.

Ezekiel 28:12-19

Son of man, take up a lamentation for the king of Tyre, and say to him, "Thus says the Lord GOD: 'You were the seal of perfection, full of wisdom and perfect in beauty. You were in Eden, the garden of God; every precious stone was your covering: the sardius, topaz, and diamond, Beryl, onyx, and jasper, sapphire, turquoise, and emerald with gold. The workmanship of your timbrels and pipes was prepared for you on the day you were created. You were the anointed cherub who covers; I established you; you were on the holy mountain of God; you walked back and forth in the midst of fiery stones. You were perfect in your ways from the day you were created, till iniquity was found in you. By the abundance of your trading you became filled with violence within, and you sinned; therefore I cast you as a profane thing out of the mountain of God; and I destroyed you, O covering cherub, from the midst of the fiery stones. Your heart was lifted up because of your beauty; you corrupted your wisdom for the sake of your splendor; I cast you to the ground, I laid you before kings, that they might gaze at you. You defiled your sanctuaries by the multitude of your iniquities, by the iniquity of your trading; therefore I brought fire from your midst; it devoured you, and I turned you to ashes upon the earth in the sight of all who saw you. All who knew you among the peoples are astonished at you; you have become a horror, and shall be no more forever.'"

Mark 16:17-18
And these signs will follow those who believe: In My name they will cast out demons; they will speak with new tongues; they will take up serpents; and if they drink anything deadly, it will by no means hurt them; they will lay hands on the sick, and they will recover."

Luke 10:19
Behold, I give you the authority to trample on serpents and scorpions, and over all the power of the enemy, and nothing shall by any means hurt you.

II Corinthians 11:14
And no wonder! For Satan himself transforms himself into an angel of light.

Ephesians 4:27
. . . nor give place to the devil.

Ephesians 6:11-12
Put on the whole armor of God, that you may be able to stand against the wiles of the devil. For we do not wrestle against flesh and blood, but against principalities, against powers, against the rulers of the darkness of this age, against spiritual hosts of wickedness in the heavenly places.

James 4:7
Therefore submit to God. Resist the devil and he will flee from you.

I Peter 5:8
Be sober, be vigilant; because your adversary the devil walks about like a roaring lion, seeking whom he may devour.

I John 4:4
You are of God, little children, and have overcome them, because He who is in you is greater than he who is in the world.

Revelation 12:9-11
So the great dragon was cast out, that serpent of old, called the Devil and Satan, who deceives the whole world; he was cast to the earth, and his angels were cast out with him. Then I heard a loud voice saying in heaven, "Now salvation, and strength, and the kingdom of our God, and the power of His Christ have come, for the accuser of our brethren, who accused them before our God day and night, has been cast down. And they overcame him by the blood of the Lamb and by the word of their testimony, and they did not love their lives to the death."

RENEWAL THOUGHT
We are to resist the devil, not submit to him.

SECOND COMING
OF CHRIST

When Jesus returns, He is going to come to earth from heaven with a shout, with the voice of the archangel, and with the trump of God. He is going to have all the saints, all the Christian men and women who have died, with Him.

So Jesus is coming. The spirits and souls of all the Christians who have already died will be with Him. Their physical bodies will come up out of the ground and be recreated into their spiritual bodies. The spirits and souls will meet the spiritual bodies and will be together throughout eternity with Jesus. Those still living will be changed in the twinkling of an eye and receive recreated, glorified bodies. They will then meet the Lord in the air to also be with Him throughout eternity.

<u>Setting Your Course</u>, Casey Treat

Matthew 24:14, 36-42
And this gospel of the kingdom will be preached in all the world as a witness to all the nations, and then the end will come. But of that day and hour no one knows, not even the angels of heaven, but My Father only. But as the days of Noah were, so also will the coming of the Son of Man be. For as in the days before the flood, they were eating and drinking, marrying and giving in marriage, until the day that Noah entered the ark, and did not know until the flood came and took them all away, so also will the coming of the Son of Man be. Then two

men will be in the field: one will be taken and the other left. Two women will be grinding at the mill: one will be taken and the other left. Watch therefore, for you do not know what hour your Lord is coming.

Matthew 25:1-13

Then the kingdom of heaven shall be likened to ten virgins who took their lamps and went out to meet the bridegroom. Now five of them were wise, and five were foolish. Those who were foolish took their lamps and took no oil with them, but the wise took oil in their vessels with their lamps. But while the bridegroom was delayed, they all slumbered and slept. And at midnight a cry was heard: "Behold, the bridegroom is coming; go out to meet him!" Then all those virgins arose and trimmed their lamps. And the foolish said to the wise, "Give us some of your oil, for our lamps are going out." But the wise answered, saying, "No, lest there should not be enough for us and you; but go rather to those who sell, and buy for yourselves." And while they went to buy, the bridegroom came, and those who were ready went in with him to the wedding; and the door was shut. Afterward the other virgins came also, saying, "Lord, Lord, open to us!" But he answered and said, "Assuredly, I say to you, I do not know you." Watch therefore, for you know neither the day nor the hour in which the Son of Man is coming.

Luke 19:11-13

Now as they heard these things, He spoke another parable, because He was near Jerusalem and because they thought the kingdom of God would appear immediately. Therefore He said: "A certain nobleman went into a far country to receive for himself a kingdom and to return. So he called ten of his servants, delivered to them ten minas, and said to them, 'Do business till I come.'"

Acts 1:9-11

Now when He had spoken these things, while they watched, He was taken up, and a cloud received Him out of their sight. And while they looked steadfastly toward heaven as He went up, behold, two men stood by them in white apparel, who also said, "Men of Galilee, why do you stand gazing up into heaven? This same Jesus, who was taken up from you into heaven, will so come in like manner as you saw Him go into heaven."

I Thessalonians 4:14-18

For if we believe that Jesus died and rose again, even so God will bring with Him those who sleep in Jesus. For this we say to you by the word of the Lord, that we who are alive and remain until the coming of the Lord will by no means precede those who are asleep. For the Lord Himself will descend from heaven with a shout, with the voice of an archangel, and with the trumpet of God. And the dead in Christ will rise first. Then we who are alive and remain shall be caught up together with them in the clouds to meet the Lord in the air. And thus we shall always be with the Lord. Therefore comfort one another with these words.

I Thessalonians 5:1-4
But concerning the times and the seasons, brethren, you have no need that I should write to you. For you yourselves know perfectly that the day of the Lord so comes as a thief in the night. For when they say, "Peace and safety!" then sudden destruction comes upon them, as labor pains upon a pregnant woman. And they shall not escape. But you, brethren, are not in darkness, so that this Day should overtake you as a thief.

RENEWAL THOUGHT
The second coming will be sudden, and the big question is: Who will be ready?

SELF-IMAGE

If you will get back to knowing who you are and what God says about you, if you will believe what God says more than what society says, more than what the government or a philosopher or a counselor says, then and only then will you rise to your full potential and experience your God-given destiny. Believe what God says about you! Then you will rise to the high level of life that is possible for you as a creation of God.

Some religions tell you that you're nothing but a worm or a dog. You're just dirt. They heap guilt and condemnation on you. But God says to you, "My child, lift up your head and come boldly unto the throne of grace where you will find mercy and help in your time of need." God crowns us with glory and honor.

<u>Fulfilling Your God-Given Destiny</u>, Casey Treat

Genesis 1:26-28
Then God said, "Let Us make man in Our image, according to Our likeness; let them have dominion over the fish of the sea, over the birds of the air, and over the cattle, over all the earth and over every creeping thing that creeps on the earth." So God created man in His own image; in the image of God He created him; male and female He created them. Then God blessed them, and God said to them, "Be fruitful and multiply; fill the earth and subdue it; have dominion over the fish of the sea, over the birds of the air, and over every living thing that moves on the earth."

Judges 6:11-12
Now the Angel of the LORD came and sat under the terebinth tree which was in Ophrah, which belonged to Joash the Abiezrite, while his son Gideon threshed wheat in the winepress, in order to hide it from the Midianites. And the Angel of the LORD appeared to him, and said to him, "The LORD is with you, you mighty man of valor!"

Psalm 8:4-6
What is man that You are mindful of him, and the son of man that You visit him? For You have made him a little lower than the angels, and You have crowned him with glory and honor. You have made him to have dominion over the works of Your hands; you have put all things under his feet.

Romans 8:37
Yet in all these things we are more than conquerors through Him who loved us.

Romans 12:3
For I say, through the grace given to me, to everyone who is among you, not to think of himself more highly than he ought to think, but to think soberly, as God has dealt to each one a measure of faith.

Philippians 4:8
Finally, brethren, whatever things are true, whatever things are noble, whatever things are just, whatever things are pure, whatever things are lovely, whatever things are of good report, if there is any virtue and if there is anything praiseworthy— meditate on these things.

Philippians 4:13
I can do all things through Christ who strengthens me.

I John 4:4
You are of God, little children, and have overcome them, because He who is in you is greater than he who is in the world.

RENEWAL THOUGHT
God never stops seeing us as valuable and precious, worthy to die for and worthy to live for.

Sleeping Well

God's will is that we rest and sleep with peace. As we fulfill His will every day and live by His Word, we can go to sleep with the peace of God that passes understanding.

Casey Treat

Psalm 4:8
I will both lie down in peace, and sleep; for You alone, O LORD, make me dwell in safety.

Psalm 127:2
It is vain for you to rise up early, to sit up late, to eat the bread of sorrows; for so He gives His beloved sleep.

Proverbs 3:21-24
My son, let them not depart from your eyes— keep sound wisdom and discretion; so they will be life to your soul and grace to your neck. Then you will walk safely in your way, and your foot will not stumble. When you lie down, you will not be afraid; yes, you will lie down and your sleep will be sweet.

Proverbs 20:13
Do not love sleep, lest you come to poverty; open your eyes, and you will be satisfied with bread.

Renewal Thought
When we live right and do right during the day, sleeping at night will be blessed and peaceful.

SPEECH

Y ou are having exactly what you have been saying. If you have been saying, "I'm so sick and tired, I don't like this. I'm so tired of this," then that's what you will have. We have a spirit of faith; not a griping spirit, a murmuring spirit, or a lazy spirit, but a spirit of faith.

If you see a problem, speak a change into it. Don't complain about it. Speak life into it and speak good things into it. When you have a spirit of faith and a positive confession it will cause you to overcome in Jesus' name.

Casey Treat

Psalm 37:30
The mouth of the righteous speaks wisdom, and his tongue talks of justice.

Psalm 145:11
They shall speak of the glory of Your kingdom, and talk of Your power.

Proverbs 16:24
Pleasant words are like a honeycomb, sweetness to the soul and health to the bones.

Proverbs 10:11
The mouth of the righteous is a well of life, but violence covers the mouth of the wicked.

Proverbs 25:11

A word fitly spoken is like apples of gold in settings of silver.

Ecclesiastes 10:12

The words of a wise man's mouth are gracious, but the lips of a fool shall swallow him up.

Isaiah 50:4

The Lord GOD has given Me the tongue of the learned, that I should know how to speak a word in season to him who is weary. He awakens Me morning by morning, he awakens My ear to hear as the learned.

Matthew 5:37

But let your "Yes" be "Yes," and your "No," "No." For whatever is more than these is from the evil one.

Ephesians 5:19

. . . speaking to one another in psalms and hymns and spiritual songs, singing and making melody in your heart to the Lord.

Colossians 4:6

Let your speech always be with grace, seasoned with salt, that you may know how you ought to answer each one.

II Timothy 1:13

Hold fast the pattern of sound words which you have heard from me, in faith and love which are in Christ Jesus.

Titus 2:8

. . . sound speech that cannot be condemned, that one who is an opponent may be ashamed, having nothing evil to say of you.

James 3:2

For we all stumble in many things. If anyone does not stumble in word, he is a perfect man, able also to bridle the whole body.

RENEWAL THOUGHT

What's in your heart comes out of your mouth.

STRENGTH

Joshua 1:6 says: "Be strong and of good courage. . ." That's a commandment. God doesn't say "try." God didn't say be strong if you feel like it. He said, "Be strong and of good courage." Not only do we need to be strong, but we also need to be VERY COURAGEOUS. God knows that if you're not strong and courageous the devil is going to overpower you. He's going to put a spirit of fear on you.

Start thinking strongly. Start thinking courageously. Start to think that YOU CAN DO ALL THINGS THROUGH CHRIST WHO STRENGTHENS YOU!

Casey Treat

Psalm 18:1-2
I will love You, O LORD, my strength. The LORD is my rock and my fortress and my deliverer; my God, my strength, in whom I will trust; my shield and the horn of my salvation, my stronghold.

Psalm 27:1
The LORD is my light and my salvation; whom shall I fear? The LORD is the strength of my life; of whom shall I be afraid?

Isaiah 40:28-31
Have you not known? Have you not heard? The everlasting God, the LORD, the Creator of the ends of the earth, neither faints nor is weary. His understanding is unsearchable. He gives power to the

weak, and to those who have no might He increases strength. Even the youths shall faint and be weary, and the young men shall utterly fall, but those who wait on the LORD shall renew their strength; they shall mount up with wings like eagles, they shall run and not be weary, they shall walk and not faint.

Joel 3:10
Beat your plowshares into swords and your pruning hooks into spears; let the weak say, "I am strong."

Romans 4:19-21
And not being weak in faith, he did not consider his own body, already dead (since he was about a hundred years old), and the deadness of Sarah's womb. He did not waver at the promise of God through unbelief, but was strengthened in faith, giving glory to God, and being fully convinced that what He had promised He was also able to perform.

II Corinthians 12:9-10
And He said to me, "My grace is sufficient for you, for My strength is made perfect in weakness." Therefore most gladly I will rather boast in my infirmities, that the power of Christ may rest upon me. Therefore I take pleasure in infirmities, in reproaches, in needs, in persecutions, in distresses, for Christ's sake. For when I am weak, then I am strong.

Ephesians 6:10
Finally, my brethren, be strong in the Lord and in the power of His might.

Philippians 4:13
I can do all things through Christ who strengthens me.

RENEWAL THOUGHT

You may not feel strong and courageous today. But that doesn't mean you aren't.

SUCCESS

$\mathbb{T}$he exciting thing about your destiny is that it was designed in the counsel of God's will (Ephesians 1:11). He created you for a purpose. God had a person or people that He needed to affect in some way. And so you were born. It's not that you were born and then God came up with something for you to do. God had something for you to do before the foundation of the world. You were born to do it. Your purpose was established - then your existence was established. God has a productive life planned for you, a life of meaning and purpose that will make a difference in others' lives and in His kingdom. It may be to affect one person or family who then go on to affect many others. It may be to raise great kids and then help other parents do the same. (What a tremendous need in today's world!) It may be to assist someone who is touching other lives and to help make that ministry or business a success.

Fulfilling Your God-Given Destiny, Casey Treat

Joshua 1:8
This Book of the Law shall not depart from your mouth, but you shall meditate in it day and night, that you may observe to do according to all that is written in it. For then you will make your way prosperous, and then you will have good success.

Psalm 1:1-3
Blessed is the man who walks not in the counsel of

the ungodly, nor stands in the path of sinners, nor sits in the seat of the scornful; but his delight is in the law of the LORD, and in His law he meditates day and night. He shall be like a tree planted by the rivers of water, that brings forth its fruit in its season, whose leaf also shall not wither; and whatever he does shall prosper.

Isaiah 41:10
Fear not, for I am with you; be not dismayed, for I am your God. I will strengthen you, yes, I will help you, I will uphold you with My righteous right hand.

II Corinthians 3:6
. . . who also made us sufficient as ministers of the new covenant, not of the letter but of the Spirit; for the letter kills, but the Spirit gives life.

II Corinthians 9:8
And God is able to make all grace abound toward you, that you, always having all sufficiency in all things, may have an abundance for every good work.

Philippians 4:13
I can do all things through Christ who strengthens me.

I Timothy 1:12
And I thank Christ Jesus our Lord who has enabled me, because He counted me faithful, putting me into the ministry.

III John 2
Beloved, I pray that you may prosper in all things
and be in health, just as your soul prospers.

RENEWAL THOUGHT

*One thing you should know for sure: God has not
planned a barely-get-by, mediocre, mundane life for
you.*

SUFFERING

There are times of struggle and despair in every life. There are times of sowing and times of reaping. We all go through winters before we enjoy the summer, but God planned for every one of us to bring forth good fruit throughout our lifetime. God is a good shepherd, not an evil one. If we walk with Him we shall not want. There will be valleys that we go through - even the valley of the shadow of death. But He will not leave us there. We never camp in the valley. We go through it to reach our destiny.

Fulfilling Your God-Given Destiny, Casey Treat

Romans 8:17-18
. . . and if children, then heirs— heirs of God and joint heirs with Christ, if indeed we suffer with Him, that we may also be glorified together. For I consider that the sufferings of this present time are not worthy to be compared with the glory which shall be revealed in us.

Philippians 3:10
. . . that I may know Him and the power of His resurrection, and the fellowship of His sufferings, being conformed to His death.

I Peter 4:12-16
Beloved, do not think it strange concerning the fiery trial which is to try you, as though some strange thing happened to you; but rejoice to the extent that

you partake of Christ's sufferings, that when His glory is revealed, you may also be glad with exceeding joy. If you are reproached for the name of Christ, blessed are you, for the Spirit of glory and of God rests upon you. On their part He is blasphemed, but on your part He is glorified. But let none of you suffer as a murderer, a thief, an evildoer, or as a busybody in other people's matters. Yet if anyone suffers as a Christian, let him not be ashamed, but let him glorify God in this matter.

I Peter 5:10
But may the God of all grace, who called us to His eternal glory by Christ Jesus, after you have suffered a while, perfect, establish, strengthen, and settle you.

RENEWAL THOUGHT
The runner can go through the pain and the hardships of training if he focuses on the prize of winning the race.

TEMPTATION

James says we are not to think that God is sending us testings and temptations. This is a theological position that many Christians have a mistaken belief about. They think God is sending temptations and problems. Let no man say when he is tempted, tested and tried that God sent it!

Now don't get me wrong. When Satan comes to tempt or to test, God certainly can and does use that to teach us. But God doesn't send the devil. God is not sending Satan to your life to try to humble you or teach you or keep you under control. God teaches us by His Word. He teaches us by His apostles, prophets, evangelists, pastors and teachers. He teaches us through one another. He doesn't send Satan to teach us!

<u>The Benefits of Godly Wisdom</u>, Casey Treat

Matthew 4:1-4
Then Jesus was led up by the Spirit into the wilderness to be tempted by the devil. And when He had fasted forty days and forty nights, afterward He was hungry. Now when the tempter came to Him, he said, "If You are the Son of God, command that these stones become bread." But He answered and said, "It is written, 'Man shall not live by bread alone, but by every word that proceeds from the mouth of God.'"

I Corinthians 7:5

Do not deprive one another except with consent for a time, that you may give yourselves to fasting and prayer; and come together again so that Satan does not tempt you because of your lack of self-control.

I Corinthians 10:13

No temptation has overtaken you except such as is common to man; but God is faithful, who will not allow you to be tempted beyond what you are able, but with the temptation will also make the way of escape, that you may be able to bear it.

James 1:2-4

My brethren, count it all joy when you fall into various trials, knowing that the testing of your faith produces patience. But let patience have its perfect work, that you may be perfect and complete, lacking nothing.

James 1:12-15

Blessed is the man who endures temptation; for when he has been approved, he will receive the crown of life which the Lord has promised to those who love Him. Let no one say when he is tempted, "I am tempted by God"; for God cannot be tempted by evil, nor does He Himself tempt anyone. But each one is tempted when he is drawn away by his own desires and enticed. Then, when desire has conceived, it gives birth to sin; and sin, when it is full-grown, brings forth death.

II Peter 2:9

. . . then the Lord knows how to deliver the godly
out of temptations and to reserve the unjust under
punishment for the day of judgment.

Renewal Thought

*The Bible says that Jesus was tempted in every-
thing that we are tempted to do. How come He
avoided it? Because of love.*

TITHING

If we move toward God and obey His Word we can expect to move into prosperity. If we eliminate God and forsake His Word we will slide into deeper and deeper debt. This is a biblical principle, and it works regardless of the environment.

Errors of the Prosperity Gospel, Casey Treat

Genesis 14:18-22
Then Melchizedek king of Salem brought out bread and wine; he was the priest of God Most High. And he blessed him and said: "Blessed be Abram of God Most High, Possessor of heaven and earth; and blessed be God Most High, who has delivered your enemies into your hand." And he gave him a tithe of all. Now the king of Sodom said to Abram, "Give me the persons, and take the goods for yourself." But Abram said to the king of Sodom, "I have raised my hand to the LORD, God Most High, the Possessor of heaven and earth."

Proverbs 3:9
Honor the LORD with your possessions, and with the firstfruits of all your increase.

Malachi 3:8-12
"Will a man rob God? Yet you have robbed Me! But you say, 'In what way have we robbed You?' In tithes and offerings. You are cursed with a curse, for you have robbed Me, even this whole nation. Bring all the tithes into the storehouse, that there may be food in My house, and try Me now in this,"

says the LORD of hosts, "If I will not open for you the windows of heaven and pour out for you such blessing that there will not be room enough to receive it. And I will rebuke the devourer for your sakes, so that he will not destroy the fruit of your ground, nor shall the vine fail to bear fruit for you in the field," says the LORD of hosts; and all nations will call you blessed, for you will be a delightful land," says the LORD of hosts.

I Corinthians 16:1-2

Now concerning the collection for the saints, as I have given orders to the churches of Galatia, so you must do also: On the first day of the week let each one of you lay something aside, storing up as he may prosper, that there be no collections when I come.

RENEWAL THOUGHT

God robbers will get robbed. Tithers receive the windows of heaven, and God rebukes the devil for you, too.

Tongue Restrained

The tongue is a weapon for spiritual warfare. God knows it and the devil also knows it. Remember the old saying from World War II: "The slip of a lip could sink the ship"? The crews on submarines were put on "silence" to sneak by the enemy under water without being detected. Radar could pick up the sound of their talking, and if detected, the enemy would shoot torpedoes at the sound. If any crew member "slipped their lip" one time, the whole ship could be destroyed. Christians can let their lips slip too much. We need to remember that death and life are in the power of our tongues.
<u>Fighting for Excellence in Leadership</u>, Casey Treat

Psalm 34:13
Keep your tongue from evil, and your lips from speaking deceit.

Proverbs 13:3
He who guards his mouth preserves his life, but he who opens wide his lips shall have destruction.

Proverbs 18:21
Death and life are in the power of the tongue, and those who love it will eat its fruit.

Proverbs 21:23
Whoever guards his mouth and tongue keeps his soul from troubles.

Mark 11:13-23

And seeing from afar a fig tree having leaves, He went to see if perhaps He would find something on it. And when He came to it, He found nothing but leaves, for it was not the season for figs. In response Jesus said to it, "Let no one eat fruit from you ever again." And His disciples heard it. So they came to Jerusalem. And Jesus went into the temple and began to drive out those who bought and sold in the temple, and overturned the tables of the money changers and the seats of those who sold doves. And He would not allow anyone to carry wares through the temple. Then He taught, saying to them, "Is it not written, 'My house shall be called a house of prayer for all nations'? But you have made it a 'den of thieves.'" And the scribes and chief priests heard it and sought how they might destroy Him; for they feared Him, because all the people were astonished at His teaching. When evening had come, He went out of the city. Now in the morning, as they passed by, they saw the fig tree dried up from the roots. And Peter, remembering, said to Him, "Rabbi, look! The fig tree which You cursed has withered away." So Jesus answered and said to them, "Have faith in God. For assuredly, I say to you, whoever says to this mountain, 'Be removed and be cast into the sea,' and does not doubt in his heart, but believes that those things he says will come to pass, he will have whatever he says."

James 1:26

If anyone among you thinks he is religious, and does

not bridle his tongue but deceives his own heart, this one's religion is useless.

James 3:2-10
For we all stumble in many things. If anyone does not stumble in word, he is a perfect man, able also to bridle the whole body. Indeed, we put bits in horses' mouths that they may obey us, and we turn their whole body. Look also at ships: although they are so large and are driven by fierce winds, they are turned by a very small rudder wherever the pilot desires. Even so the tongue is a little member and boasts great things. See how great a forest a little fire kindles! And the tongue is a fire, a world of iniquity. The tongue is so set among our members that it defiles the whole body, and sets on fire the course of nature; and it is set on fire by hell. For every kind of beast and bird, of reptile and creature of the sea, is tamed and has been tamed by mankind. But no man can tame the tongue. It is an unruly evil, full of deadly poison. With it we bless our God and Father, and with it we curse men, who have been made in the similitude of God. Out of the same mouth proceed blessing and cursing. My brethren, these things ought not to be so.

I Peter 3:10
For "He who would love life and see good days, let him refrain his tongue from evil, and his lips from speaking deceit."

RENEWAL THOUGHT
We have what we say according to Jesus, be it good or evil.

TRIALS

You may have problems or circumstances that seem too difficult, but you can be ready for anything and equal to anything with which the devil or the world can come against you. You are of God and have already overcome the spirit of antichrist, because the Holy Spirit within you is greater than anything else in the world.

Blueprint for Life, Casey Treat

I Corinthians 10:13
No temptation has overtaken you except such as is common to man; but God is faithful, who will not allow you to be tempted beyond what you are able, but with the temptation will also make the way of escape, that you may be able to bear it.

James 1:2-4
My brethren, count it all joy when you fall into various trials, knowing that the testing of your faith produces patience. But let patience have its perfect work, that you may be perfect and complete, lacking nothing.

I Peter 1:7-8
. . . that the genuineness of your faith, being much more precious than gold that perishes, though it is tested by fire, may be found to praise, honor, and glory at the revelation of Jesus Christ, whom having not seen you love. Though now you do not see

Him, yet believing, you rejoice with joy inexpressible and full of glory.

I Peter 4:12-13
Beloved, do not think it strange concerning the fiery trial which is to try you, as though some strange thing happened to you; but rejoice to the extent that you partake of Christ's sufferings, that when His glory is revealed, you may also be glad with exceeding joy.

RENEWAL THOUGHT
God has given us the principles and the power to live above the problems of this world.

TRINITY

God is the Father, the Son, and the Holy Spirit
- but He is One God. He works in complete unity.
You cannot separate the Father, the Son, and the
Holy Spirit. The three Persons of the trinity are all
One.

Reaching Your Destiny, Casey Treat

Genesis 1:26
Then God said, "Let Us make man in Our image,
according to Our likeness; let them have dominion
over the fish of the sea, over the birds of the air,
and over the cattle, over all the earth and over every creeping thing that creeps on the earth."

Matthew 3:16-17
When He had been baptized, Jesus came up immediately from the water; and behold, the heavens
were opened to Him, and He saw the Spirit of God
descending like a dove and alighting upon Him.
And suddenly a voice came from heaven, saying,
"This is My beloved Son, in whom I am well
pleased."

Matthew 28:19
Go therefore and make disciples of all the nations,
baptizing them in the name of the Father and of the
Son and of the Holy Spirit.

John 10:30
I and My Father are one.

II Corinthians 13:14
The grace of the Lord Jesus Christ, and the love of God, and the communion of the Holy Spirit be with you all. Amen.

Hebrews 1:8
But to the Son He says: "Your throne, O God, is forever and ever; a scepter of righteousness is the scepter of Your Kingdom."

RENEWAL THOUGHT
If you have One of Them, you have Them All.

TRUTH

If we have truth within us, and we are walking in truth, there is a commitment and a passion in our lifestyle. Many Christians have a half-hearted commitment to truth; therefore they have a half-hearted walk and relationship with the Lord.

Renewing the Mind, Casey Treat

Psalm 25:10
All the paths of the LORD are mercy and truth, to such as keep His covenant and His testimonies.

Psalm 119:30
I have chosen the way of truth; your judgments I have laid before me.

John 8:31-32
Then Jesus said to those Jews who believed Him, "If you abide in My word, you are My disciples indeed. And you shall know the truth, and the truth shall make you free."

John 14:6
Jesus said to him, "I am the way, the truth, and the life. No one comes to the Father except through Me."

John 17:17
Sanctify them by Your truth. Your word is truth.

Ephesians 4:15
. . . but, speaking the truth in love, may grow up in all things into Him who is the head— Christ.

Ephesians 4:25
Therefore, putting away lying, "Let each one of you speak truth with his neighbor," for we are members of one another.

II Timothy 2:15
Be diligent to present yourself approved to God, a worker who does not need to be ashamed, rightly dividing the word of truth.

Renewal Thought

To have the truth in us is to live it every day.

UNITY

When we love each other, we are like-minded. We are in one accord. We are not competing against one another. We are working together. We are not trying to overcome anyone, we are all trying to overcome the devil.

Casey Treat

Psalm 133:1
Behold, how good and how pleasant it is for brethren to dwell together in unity!

Acts 2:46-47
So continuing daily with one accord in the temple, and breaking bread from house to house, they ate their food with gladness and simplicity of heart, praising God and having favor with all the people. And the Lord added to the church daily those who were being saved.

Acts 4:24
So when they heard that, they raised their voice to God with one accord and said: "Lord, You are God, who made heaven and earth and the sea, and all that is in them."

Acts 5:12-14
And through the hands of the apostles many signs and wonders were done among the people. And they were all with one accord in Solomon's Porch. Yet none of the rest dared join them, but the people es-

teemed them highly. And believers were increasingly added to the Lord, multitudes of both men and women.

Ephesians 4:3-6,11-15

. . . endeavoring to keep the unity of the Spirit in the bond of peace. There is one body and one Spirit, just as you were called in one hope of your calling; one Lord, one faith, one baptism; one God and Father of all, who is above all, and through all, and in you all. And He Himself gave some to be apostles, some prophets, some evangelists, and some pastors and teachers, for the equipping of the saints for the work of ministry, for the edifying of the body of Christ, till we all come to the unity of the faith and of the knowledge of the Son of God, to a perfect man, to the measure of the stature of the fullness of Christ; that we should no longer be children, tossed to and fro and carried about with every wind of doctrine, by the trickery of men, in the cunning craftiness of deceitful plotting, but, speaking the truth in love, may grow up in all things into Him who is the head— Christ.

Philippians 2:1-3

Therefore if there is any consolation in Christ, if any comfort of love, if any fellowship of the Spirit, if any affection and mercy, fulfill my joy by being like-minded, having the same love, being of one accord, of one mind. Let nothing be done through selfish ambition or conceit, but in lowliness of mind let each esteem others better than himself.

RENEWAL THOUGHT

Love esteems others more highly and is in harmony with other people.

WATER BAPTISM

Baptism symbolizes a new creature, a new person, a new man, a new woman in Jesus Christ. It is saying, "I am crucified with Christ. I am raised up with Christ as a new person." You cannot get that same meaning out of sprinkling or out of any other form of baptism. Immersion and submersion is a symbol of being dead, buried, and resurrected with Christ. That's why we are baptized as an outward sign of what has happened inwardly when we are born again.

Setting Your Course, Casey Treat

Matthew 28:19
Go therefore and make disciples of all the nations, baptizing them in the name of the Father and of the Son and of the Holy Spirit.

Mark 16:16
He who believes and is baptized will be saved; but he who does not believe will be condemned.

Acts 2:38
Then Peter said to them, "Repent, and let every one of you be baptized in the name of Jesus Christ for the remission of sins; and you shall receive the gift of the Holy Spirit."

Acts 10:48
And he commanded them to be baptized in the name of the Lord. Then they asked him to stay a few days.

Acts 22:16
And now why are you waiting? Arise and be baptized, and wash away your sins, calling on the name of the Lord.

Romans 6:3-5
Or do you not know that as many of us as were baptized into Christ Jesus were baptized into His death? Therefore we were buried with Him through baptism into death, that just as Christ was raised from the dead by the glory of the Father, even so we also should walk in newness of life. For if we have been united together in the likeness of His death, certainly we also shall be in the likeness of His resurrection.

I Corinthians 12:13
For by one Spirit we were all baptized into one body— whether Jews or Greeks, whether slaves or free— and have all been made to drink into one Spirit.

Galatians 3:27
For as many of you as were baptized into Christ have put on Christ.

Colossians 2:12
. . . buried with Him in baptism, in which you also were raised with Him through faith in the working of God, who raised Him from the dead.

RENEWAL THOUGHT

You are not baptized so that your sins will be remitted. You are baptized because your sins are remitted.

WISDOM

There is a progression in Proverbs that is a key to gaining wisdom. We start with knowledge and grow to understanding. Then we begin to act in wisdom.

You can know whether a person has wisdom by what they do. The wise person is someone who is acting on knowledge and understanding with prudence and good judgment. They are producing good results.

<u>The Benefits of Godly Wisdom</u>, Casey Treat

Proverbs 1:5
A wise man will hear and increase learning, and a man of understanding will attain wise counsel.

Proverbs 3:13-19
Happy is the man who finds wisdom, and the man who gains understanding; for her proceeds are better than the profits of silver, and her gain than fine gold. She is more precious than rubies, and all the things you may desire cannot compare with her. Length of days is in her right hand, in her left hand riches and honor. Her ways are ways of pleasantness, and all her paths are peace. She is a tree of life to those who take hold of her, and happy are all who retain her. The LORD by wisdom founded the earth; by understanding He established the heavens.

Proverbs 4:7-8
Wisdom is the principal thing; therefore get wisdom. And in all your getting, get understanding. Exalt her, and she will promote you; she will bring you honor, when you embrace her.

Proverbs 9:8-10
Do not correct a scoffer, lest he hate you; rebuke a wise man, and he will love you. Give instruction to a wise man, and he will be still wiser; teach a just man, and he will increase in learning. "The fear of the LORD is the beginning of wisdom, and the knowledge of the Holy One is understanding."

Proverbs 11:14
Where there is no counsel, the people fall; but in the multitude of counselors there is safety.

Proverbs 29:15
The rod and rebuke give wisdom, but a child left to himself brings shame to his mother.

I Corinthians 1:30
But of Him you are in Christ Jesus, who became for us wisdom from God— and righteousness and sanctification and redemption.

James 1:5-8
If any of you lacks wisdom, let him ask of God, who gives to all liberally and without reproach, and it will be given to him. But let him ask in faith, with no doubting, for he who doubts is like a wave of the sea driven and tossed by the wind. For let

not that man suppose that he will receive anything from the Lord; he is a double-minded man, unstable in all his ways.

RENEWAL THOUGHT

Wisdom is the putting to work of knowledge and understanding, and that comes from God.

WIVES

We women need to understand how important we are in building up our husbands. It is important what we think and what we feel about our husbands. Are we building them up or are we pushing them down? When your husband walks in from work, how do you treat him? Do you stay sitting down and yell, "I'm sure glad you're home! Finally I'll get some help!" Or do you even notice that he's come home? You are running after kids; cooking the dinner; busy doing something else. Do you remember to take a moment and say, "Hey, I'm so glad you're home. How was your day?"

<u>Battle of the Sexes</u>, Wendy Treat

Proverbs 31:10-31
Who can find a virtuous wife? For her worth is far above rubies. The heart of her husband safely trusts her; so he will have no lack of gain. She does him good and not evil all the days of her life. She seeks wool and flax, and willingly works with her hands. She is like the merchant ships, she brings her food from afar. She also rises while it is yet night, and provides food for her household, and a portion for her maidservants. She considers a field and buys it; from her profits she plants a vineyard. She girds herself with strength, and strengthens her arms. She perceives that her merchandise is good, and her lamp does not go out by night. She stretches out her hands to the distaff, and her hand holds the spindle. She extends her hand to the poor, yes, she

reaches out her hands to the needy. She is not afraid of snow for her household, for all her household is clothed with scarlet. She makes tapestry for herself; her clothing is fine linen and purple. Her husband is known in the gates, when he sits among the elders of the land. She makes linen garments and sells them, and supplies sashes for the merchants. Strength and honor are her clothing; she shall rejoice in time to come. She opens her mouth with wisdom, and on her tongue is the law of kindness. She watches over the ways of her household, and does not eat the bread of idleness. Her children rise up and call her blessed; her husband also, and he praises her: "Many daughters have done well, but you excel them all." Charm is deceitful and beauty is passing, but a woman who fears the LORD, she shall be praised. Give her of the fruit of her hands, and let her own works praise her in the gates.

Ephesians 5:22
Wives, submit to your own husbands, as to the Lord.

I Timothy 3:11
Likewise their wives must be reverent, not slanderers, temperate, faithful in all things.

I Peter 3:1
Wives, likewise, be submissive to your own husbands, that even if some do not obey the word, they, without a word, may be won by the conduct of their wives.

RENEWAL THOUGHT

God's woman will allow the Word to be big within her and will console, help, and be a strengthening aid to her husband.

WORD

Ⅰou must dedicate yourself to believing and then living the Word of God. A lot of people say they are committed to the Bible and say they believe the Bible, but their commitment consists of having the Bible sit on the coffee table, and they look at it religiously. A true New Testament believer needs to have a commitment to live the Bible.

<u>Setting Your Course</u>, Casey Treat

Psalm 25:5
Lead me in Your truth and teach me, for You are the God of my salvation; on You I wait all the day.

Psalm 107:20
He sent His word and healed them, and delivered them from their destructions.

Psalm 119:11,16
Your word I have hidden in my heart, that I might not sin against You! I will delight myself in Your statutes; I will not forget Your word.

Proverbs 4:20-22
My son, give attention to my words; incline your ear to my sayings. Do not let them depart from your eyes; keep them in the midst of your heart; for they are life to those who find them, and health to all their flesh.

Matthew 4:4

But He answered and said, "It is written, 'Man shall not live by bread alone, but by every word that proceeds from the mouth of God.'"

Matthew 5:17-19

Do not think that I came to destroy the Law or the Prophets. I did not come to destroy but to fulfill. For assuredly, I say to you, till heaven and earth pass away, one jot or one tittle will by no means pass from the law till all is fulfilled. Whoever therefore breaks one of the least of these commandments, and teaches men so, shall be called least in the kingdom of heaven; but whoever does and teaches them, he shall be called great in the kingdom of heaven.

John 1:1-5,14

In the beginning was the Word, and the Word was with God, and the Word was God. He was in the beginning with God. All things were made through Him, and without Him nothing was made that was made. In Him was life, and the life was the light of men. And the light shines in the darkness, and the darkness did not comprehend it. And the Word became flesh and dwelt among us, and we beheld His glory, the glory as of the only begotten of the Father, full of grace and truth.

John 8:31-32

Then Jesus said to those Jews who believed Him, "If you abide in My word, you are My disciples indeed. And you shall know the truth, and the truth shall make you free."

John 17:17
Sanctify them by Your truth. Your word is truth.

II Timothy 4:1-4
I charge you therefore before God and the Lord
Jesus Christ, who will judge the living and the dead
at His appearing and His kingdom: Preach the
word! Be ready in season and out of season. Convince, rebuke, exhort, with all longsuffering and
teaching. For the time will come when they will
not endure sound doctrine, but according to their
own desires, because they have itching ears, they
will heap up for themselves teachers; and they will
turn their ears away from the truth, and be turned
aside to fables.

Hebrews 4:12
For the word of God is living and powerful, and
sharper than any two-edged sword, piercing even
to the division of soul and spirit, and of joints and
marrow, and is a discerner of the thoughts and intents of the heart.

I Peter 1:23-25
. . . having been born again, not of corruptible seed
but incorruptible, through the word of God which
lives and abides forever, because "All flesh is as
grass, and all the glory of man as the flower of the
grass. The grass withers, and its flower falls away,
but the word of the Lord endures forever." Now
this is the word which by the gospel was preached
to you.

I Peter 2:2
As newborn babes, desire the pure milk of the word,
that you may grow thereby.

RENEWAL THOUGHT
God's Word is the truth, which is the basis for all
success in life.

WORRY

Jesus said we will have enough to worry about tomorrow, so do not try to pile tomorrow's worries on today. Wait until tomorrow comes and then take care of it.

His message was, "Do not worry about life. Take no anxious thought, do not get 'uptight,' do not get nervous. Trust God."

<u>Blueprint for Life</u>, Casey Treat

Job 3:25
For the thing I greatly feared has come upon me, and what I dreaded has happened to me.

Psalm 37:1-3,7
Do not fret because of evildoers, nor be envious of the workers of iniquity. For they shall soon be cut down like the grass, and wither as the green herb. Trust in the LORD, and do good; dwell in the land, and feed on His faithfulness. Rest in the LORD, and wait patiently for Him; do not fret because of him who prospers in his way, because of the man who brings wicked schemes to pass.

Matthew 6:25-31
Therefore I say to you, do not worry about your life, what you will eat or what you will drink; nor about your body, what you will put on. Is not life more than food and the body more than clothing? Look at the birds of the air, for they neither sow nor reap nor gather into barns; yet your heavenly Father feeds them. Are you not of more value than

they? Which of you by worrying can add one cubit to his stature? So why do you worry about clothing? Consider the lilies of the field, how they grow: they neither toil nor spin; and yet I say to you that even Solomon in all his glory was not arrayed like one of these. Now if God so clothes the grass of the field, which today is, and tomorrow is thrown into the oven, will He not much more clothe you, O you of little faith? Therefore do not worry, saying, "What shall we eat?" or "What shall we drink?" or "What shall we wear?"

Philippians 4:6-8
Be anxious for nothing, but in everything by prayer and supplication, with thanksgiving, let your requests be made known to God; and the peace of God, which surpasses all understanding, will guard your hearts and minds through Christ Jesus. Finally, brethren, whatever things are true, whatever things are noble, whatever things are just, whatever things are pure, whatever things are lovely, whatever things are of good report, if there is any virtue and if there is anything praiseworthy— meditate on these things.

II Timothy 1:7
For God has not given us a spirit of fear, but of power and of love and of a sound mind.

I Peter 5:6-7
Therefore humble yourselves under the mighty hand of God, that He may exalt you in due time, casting all your care upon Him, for He cares for you.

RENEWAL THOUGHT

When I'm facing some real problems in my life, I'm going to choose to rejoice in the Lord and believe that God is at work on my behalf. You have to make that choice.

WORSHIP

What is worship? Is it bowing down, closing your eyes, lifting your hands? Is it folding your hands, singing a song or sitting very quiet? It is all of this, and even more!

Worship is more than acting a certain way, or saying the right words. Worship is an attitude of your heart. An attitude of honor, respect, love, praise, excitement. We have the privilege and opportunity to love God all the time. We worship Him and bless His Name by our act of worship in giving: financially, physically, socially, spiritually. We worship God when we are obedient to His Word. When we do what the Bible says.

God wants more than lip service. He wants our hearts to follow after Him! He wants us to bless Him with all of us, not 50%!

The Fulfilled Woman, Wendy Treat

Exodus 34:14
For you shall worship no other god, for the LORD, whose name is Jealous, is a jealous God.

I Chronicles 16:29
Give to the LORD the glory due His name; bring an offering, and come before Him. Oh, worship the LORD in the beauty of holiness!

Psalm 66:4
All the earth shall worship You and sing praises to You; they shall sing praises to Your name. Selah.

Psalm 95:6-7
Oh come, let us worship and bow down; let us kneel before the LORD our Maker. For He is our God, and we are the people of His pasture, and the sheep of His hand.

Matthew 4:10
Then Jesus said to him, "Away with you, Satan! For it is written, 'You shall worship the Lord your God, and Him only you shall serve.'"

John 4:23-24
But the hour is coming, and now is, when the true worshipers will worship the Father in spirit and truth; for the Father is seeking such to worship Him. "God is Spirit, and those who worship Him must worship in spirit and truth.

RENEWAL THOUGHT
We should be ready to worship God and to praise God among all people at any time.

BIBLE CONFESSIONS

MINISTRY

The Spirit of the Lord is upon me because He has anointed me to preach the gospel to the poor. He has sent me to heal the brokenhearted, to preach deliverance to the captives, and the recovering of sight to the blind, to set at liberty them that are bruised, and to preach the acceptable year of the Lord. Jesus is made unto me wisdom, righteousness, sanctification, and redemption. If I lack wisdom, I ask of God who gives to all men liberally and upbraids not, and it is given to me. I walk in love. The love of God is shed abroad in my heart by the Holy Ghost. I've been made in the righteousness of God in Christ. Whatever I do shall prosper, for I prosper and live in health even as my soul prospers. I tread on serpents and scorpions and over all the power of the enemy. Nothing shall by any means hurt me, for the joy of the Lord is my strength.

Nehemiah 8:10; Luke 4:18; Luke 10:19; Romans 5:5; I Corinthians 1:30; II Corinthians 5:21; III John 2

PERSONAL COMMITMENT AND DISCIPLINE

I am a disciplined man/woman of God. I give myself continually to prayer and to the ministry of the Word. I study to show myself approved unto God, a workman who needs not to be ashamed, rightly dividing the Word of truth. I am not conformed to this world, but transformed by the renewing of my mind, to prove what is that good, acceptable and perfect will of God. I am risen with Christ. I seek those things which are above where Christ sits on the right hand of God. I set my mind on things above, not on things on this earth. Whatsoever things are true, honest, just, pure, lovely, of good report, virtuous, and praiseworthy, these are the only things I fix my mind on.

I love *(spouse's name)* as Jesus loved the church, and gave Himself for it. We walk in harmony and in one accord. We've been made one by the Spirit of God. I love *(children's names)*. I train them in the way they should go, and when they are old they will not depart from it. I raise them up in the nurture and the admonition of the Lord.

My body is the temple of the Holy Ghost. There shall no evil befall me, neither shall any plague come near my dwelling. By the stripes of Jesus I am healed. I am blessed with the blessings of Abraham. I am very rich in silver and in gold. The blessing of the Lord makes me rich and He adds no sorrow to it. I prosper and live in health even as my soul prospers. As He who has called me is holy, so I am holy in all manner of life style because it is written, "Be ye holy as I am holy."

I put off concerning the former conversation, the old man, which is corrupt according to the deceitful lusts. I am renewed in the spirit of my mind and put on the new man which after God is created in righteousness and true holiness. I am strong and very courageous. The Word of God shall not depart out of my mouth, but I meditate therein day and night to observe to do according to all that is written therein. Then I make my way prosperous and then I have good success.

Genesis 2:24; Joshua 1:7-8; Proverbs 9:10; Proverbs 22:6; Acts 6:4; Romans 12:2; I Corinthians 3:16; Ephesians 4:22-24; Ephesians 5:25; Ephesians 6:4; Philippians 4:8; Colossians 3:1-2; II Timothy 2:15; I Peter 1:15-16

WISDOM, KNOWLEDGE, AND THE DIRECTION OF GOD

I do not seek after riches, wealth, or honor, but I seek for wisdom and knowledge. Wisdom and knowledge are granted unto me, and I believe You've given riches, wealth, and honor according to Your Word. Wisdom is the principal thing, therefore I get wisdom, and with all my getting I get understanding. I exalt wisdom and she promotes me. She'll bring me to honor when I embrace her.

Happy is the man who finds wisdom and the man who gets understanding, for the merchandise of it is better than the merchandise of silver, and the gain thereof than fine gold. She is more precious than rubies and all the things I can desire are not to be compared to her. Length of days is in her right hand and in her left hand is riches and honor. She is the tree of life to them that lay hold upon her. Happy is everyone who retains her. The Lord by wisdom has founded the earth, by understanding has He established the heavens. I am willing and obedient, and I eat the best the land has to offer. I seek first the kingdom of God and His righteousness, and all these other things are added unto me. I am a blessed man who walks not in the counsel of the ungodly, nor stands in the way of sinners, nor sits in the seat of the scornful. But my delight is in the law of the Lord, and in Your law do I meditate day and night. I am like a tree planted by rivers of water that brings forth fruit in season. My leaf also shall not wither and whatever I do shall prosper.

II Chronicles 1:12; Proverbs 4:7-8; Proverbs 3:13-19; Isaiah 1:19; Matthew 6:33; Psalm 1:1-3

SALVATION

1. Every person must be born again to know God and go to heaven.
   John 3:3,7,16
2. We must be born again because we all have sinned.
   Romans 3:23, 6:23
3. You cannot earn salvation.
   Ephesians 2:8-9
4. Being saved or born again is receiving Jesus Christ as your Lord (Master), and committing yourself to follow His Word.
   Romans 10:9-10; I John 2:3
5. The outward man does not change instantly, but the inward man does.
   II Corinthians 5:17
6. Being born again is only a start. Just as a child grows, you must grow by training yourself on the Word.
   Romans 10:17
   a) You must be fed regularly.
      Hebrews 10:25
   b) You must change your thinking to God's thinking to win in life.
      Romans 12:1-21
7. When doubts and fears come to mind about your salvation, reject them and realize that the Bible is what your new birth is based on, and not what you feel or think.
   Romans 10:9-10
8. You need to be baptized in water as a believer.
   Mark 16:15-17

HAVE YOU BEEN
BORN AGAIN?

The first step to a successful life is that you be born again. The Bible says in John 3:3, ". . . unless one is born again, he cannot see the kingdom of God." Every person must be born again to know God and have everlasting life.

Being born again is making Jesus the Lord of your life by making Him your master, teacher, and guide. You change from going your own way to following Jesus (Romans 10:9-10).

Just say this simple prayer: "God, I come to You in the name of Jesus. I ask You to come into my life. I confess with my mouth that Jesus is my Lord, and I believe in my heart that You have raised Him from the dead. I turn my back on sin and renounce all other religions. I am now a child of God. Thank You, Jesus, that I am saved. Amen!" You are now born again! You are forgiven of your sins and on your way to heaven.

Now you must continue to feed yourself on the Word of God so that you can grow and mature in your Christian walk. Being born again is only the first step to the abundant, victorious life God has for you. Romans 12:2 tells us not to be conformed to the world, but transformed by renewing our minds. Take time to study God's Word and receive His abundant life.

Baptism Of The Holy Spirit

1. Every person must be born again to receive the Holy Spirit.
    Romans 10:9-10; Acts 19:2
2. Who is the Holy Spirit?
    a) Teacher and Comforter (John 14:26)
    b) Power (Acts 1:8)
3. The Holy Spirit is already here for every person, and you need not wait or work for Him.
    Acts 2:38-39
4. The evidence of being filled with the Holy Spirit is speaking in tongues.
    Acts 2:4; Acts 10:45-46
5. Your mind will not understand or gain anything from tongues. (It will sound foolish and useless to the natural mind.)
    I Corinthians 14:2
    a) Speaking in tongues is an act of your will. (God will not force you to do it, nor will He do it for you.)
        I Corinthians 14:14-15
6. If you ask in faith, you will receive.
    Luke 11:13
7. Praying in tongues regularly will build (edify) or change the spirit man.
    Jude 20

ARE YOU FILLED WITH THE HOLY SPIRIT?

The Bible says that Jesus sent you the Holy Spirit to be your comforter and teacher, as well as your source of power and abundant strength. The Holy Spirit gives you the ability to be an overcomer and to live a victorious Christian life (John 14:26; Acts 1:8).

The Holy Spirit is already here for every born-again believer. You need not wait for Him or work for Him, and when you receive Him you will pray out in other tongues (Acts 2:4). Your mind will not understand or gain anything from tongues because you are speaking mysteries to God, not to man (I Corinthians 14:2). But God will not force you to pray in tongues - it is an act of your will.

Luke 11:13 says, "If you then, being evil (human), know how to give good gifts to your children, how much more will your heavenly Father give the Holy Spirit to those who ask Him!" If you ask God for the Holy Spirit in faith, you will receive. Just pray this prayer: "Father, I ask you to fill me with the Holy Spirit. I receive Him now with the evidence of praying in other tongues. I will pray out boldly in other tongues in Jesus' name."

You are now filled with the Holy Spirit and power. If you will pray in tongues on a daily basis, remembering this is an act of your will, you will edify or charge up your spirit man. You will release the power of the Holy Spirit to operate on your behalf (Jude 20).

DAILY
DEVOTIONAL:
31 DAYS TO
RENEWAL

The fact that you are reading this devotional means you are serious about renewal and change. You are one of a few people who know they can and should renew their mind and their life to be what God called you to be. Most people are stuck in the mud of mediocrity, but you are moving to God's perfect will for your life.

This devotional will help you to know your destiny, see what you can accomplish in your life, and take the steps to make it happen. Each day is a step, but will be developed over a 31 day process. Like learning to drive, where many movements and decisions become automatic and simultaneous, but must be learned individually, so learning to renew and change must be learned and developed into a lifestyle.

Change is fun and rewarding, but not easy. You can do it and you will become what God wills for you.

Each part of renewing your mind and changing your life is a daily walk. To develop the skills necessary to change, let's walk together for the next 31 days. Along the way you will:

Decide what you really want (Luke 10:38);
Learn the right thoughts (II Timothy 2:15);
Speak the right confessions (Proverbs 21:18);
Focus on your destiny (Ephesians 1:17);
Meditate on the Word (Joshua 1:8); and
Be who you want to be (Joshua 1:6); and then
Practice until it is comfortable (Philippians 2:12b).

Week One

There must be clear desires and vision to move forward in transformation. Your strength to push through old habits, your energy to keep going when it seems too hard, and your focus to know where you are going are all dependent on these three things: DESIRE, VISION, and A SENSE OF DESTINY.

DESIRE - What do you want for your life?

Desire is a very powerful force in your life. You must want it deeply to go after something significant. God gives you the desires of your heart (Psalm 37:4). He uses the force of desire to direct your life and move you toward destiny - His plan for you. There is a reason you want things that others don't, and other people want things that you don't. It all has to do with God working through desires.

Desires are thoughts that create feelings and motivation to do, obtain or accomplish. They are not fantasies, trips or passing fancies. Desires come from the heart and are strong motivational factors in our lives. Satan and the world would like to pervert your desires to be unnatural, negative and carnal. Then the God-given power of desire is used to do, obtain or accomplish negative and ungodly things. Negative desires are not natural to you; you want what is good, right and godly. So go for it!!! What is the desire of your heart?

1. What are the three things you really want changed in your life?

2. What three things do you really want to accomplish in your lifetime?

Stop here for a few minutes and write the answers to these questions. Write down what you believe and feel today. It may change as we walk together for the next 31 days, but that's okay; start where you are and begin to examine what you really want, what are your desires for your life. Make sure they are your own and not your parents', spouse's or friends'. Now's the time to take a step toward change. This is where it starts; write the three greatest desires for change and three greatest desires for your future.

VISION - What will your future look like?

Vision is that internal picture of what the future looks like. It's the ability to see what you desire before it is manifested in the physical realm. The architect has a vision of the house before it is built. The artist has a vision of the picture before it is painted. God told Joshua to "see" Jericho was in his control while it was still shut up and prepared for battle. You have the ability to see your future before you get there.

God desires you to see your future so you will begin to move toward it. Have you ever experienced driving off the road in your car because you were looking at something on the side of the road? Wherever we focus our vision, we move toward. If you focus on your debt, pain and problems, you subconsciously continue to move toward them. People usually do not change because they can't see anything else for their lives.

Have you ever said something like, "I could never see myself living in that big house or driving that nice car"? If you can't see yourself doing something, it is very likely you never will.

You have the God-given ability to have a vision. Start to think about what you wrote down for your greatest desires. What would your life look like, feel like, and be like if those things were so now?

For the next few minutes, think about your life as it could be when God gives you the desires of your heart.

1. What will it look like?
2. What will be different?
3. What will it feel like?

Scriptures to meditate on:

Day 1
Psalm 37:4 - Delight yourself also in the LORD, and <u>He shall give you the desires of your heart</u>.

Day 2
Luke 10:38-42 - Now it happened as they went that He entered a certain village; and a certain woman named Martha welcomed Him into her house. And she had a sister called Mary, who also sat at Jesus' feet and heard His word. But Martha was distracted with much serving, and she approached Him and said, "Lord, do You not care that my sister has left me to serve alone? Therefore tell her to help me." And Jesus answered and said to her, "Martha, Martha, <u>you are worried and troubled about many</u>

things. "But one thing is needed, and Mary has chosen that good part, which will not be taken away from her."

Day 3
Mark 11:24 (KJV) - Therefore I say unto you, <u>What things soever ye desire</u>, when ye pray, believe that ye receive them, and ye shall have them.

Day 4
Mark 10:51-52 - So Jesus answered and said to him, "<u>What do you want Me to do for you</u>?" The blind man said to Him, "Rabboni, that I may receive my sight." Then Jesus said to him, "<u>Go your way; your faith has made you well</u>." And immediately he received his sight and followed Jesus on the road.

Day 5
Acts 2:17-18 - And it shall come to pass in the last days, says God, that I will pour out of My Spirit on all flesh; your sons and your daughters shall prophesy, <u>your young men shall see visions, your old men shall dream dreams</u>. And on My menservants and on My <u>maidservants I will pour out My Spirit</u> in those days; and they shall prophesy.

Day 6
Habakkuk 2:2-3 - Then the LORD answered me and said: "<u>Write the vision and make it plain</u> on tablets, that he may run who reads it. For the vision is yet for an appointed time; but at the end it will speak, and it will not lie. Though it tarries, wait for it; because it will surely come, it will not tarry."

Day 7

Ephesians 1:11,16-18 - In Him also we have obtained an inheritance, <u>being predestined according to the purpose of Him who works all things according to the counsel of His will</u>, that we who first trusted in Christ should be to the praise of His glory. In Him you also trusted, after you heard the word of truth, the gospel of your salvation; in whom also, having believed, you were sealed with the Holy Spirit of promise, who is the guarantee of our inheritance until the redemption of the purchased possession, to the praise of His glory. Therefore I also, after I heard of your faith in the Lord Jesus and your love for all the saints, do not cease to give thanks for you, making mention of you in my prayers: that the God of our Lord Jesus Christ, <u>the Father of glory, may give to you the spirit of wisdom and revelation in the knowledge of Him, the eyes of your understanding being enlightened; that you may know what is the hope of His calling</u>, what are the riches of the glory of His inheritance in the saints. . .

WEEK TWO

DESTINY - What has God planned for you?

God had planned a wonderful life for you even before He made the earth. Ephesians 1:3-6 says, "Blessed be the God and Father of our Lord Jesus Christ, who has blessed us with every spiritual blessing in the heavenly places in Christ, just as He chose us in Him before the foundation of the world, that we should be holy and without blame before Him in love, having predestined us to adoption as sons by Jesus Christ to Himself, according to the good pleasure of His will, to the praise of the glory of His grace, by which He has made us accepted in the Beloved." Knowing your gifts, talents and, most importantly, your desires, He established a destiny for you. He will not take control of your life; you are a free will agent made in His likeness and image. He made His plan based on your will and desires (Romans 8:29). But He has set a path, a course that is the most exciting, rewarding, and fulfilling life that you could ever find.

You have a sense of what that destiny is in your heart. As a Christian there is a witness of the Spirit as to God's will and plan for you. As you plug into your desires, you are discovering your course of destiny.

Here are ten questions to help you sort out what God has called you to. I pray you will have a spirit of wisdom and revelation in the knowledge of God, the eyes of your understanding being enlightened that you will know the hope of your calling (Ephesians 1:16-18). The Holy Spirit will help you know your destiny as you think about and answer these questions:

1. What is the deepest desire of your heart?
2. What stirs your passion?
3. What flows naturally out of you?
4. Where do you bring forth fruit or produce good results?
5. What is the witness of the Holy Spirit in your spirit?

6. What do mature Christians see in you?
7. What career or ministry do you feel the peace of God about pursuing?
8. What thoughts, visions, or dreams are impossible to put out of your mind?
9. To what can you give 100 percent of yourself for your whole life?
10. What do people want to gather around and help you accomplish?

This week go over these three words, DESIRE, VISION, and DESTINY, and the answers you have found inside yourself for each area. Think about them, rewrite them, and change them as you feel you should. These are the first steps in change and to the fulfillment of your destiny. With desires, vision, and a sense of destiny alive in your heart and mind, you are on your way to a higher level of life.

MEDITATE - As you focus your thoughts on what you want and where you are going, you will begin to move toward it.

During this second week we want to break some old habits of thinking. Proverbs 23:7 tells us, "As a man thinks in his heart so is he." You are in your current situations because of the way you think about certain things. You get stuck in those circumstances because the same thoughts continue to dominate your mind. We can't change our thinking by trying not to think about something. We change our thinking by focusing on new thoughts and developing a new way of thinking.

The person who wants to loose weight must change their thoughts about food and exercise.

However, you can't do that by taking a diet pill or trying fad diets. You must develop a new way of thinking about food, why you eat, when you eat and what you eat, and new thoughts about exercise so you can change and be fit.

Meditation is something you do everyday. We all meditate, but we usually don't think about what we're thinking about. We spend hours thinking about what we don't like or don't want in our lives, but we don't meditate on what we do want and what we will like. Remember, whatever you focus your thoughts on you begin to move toward.

This week remind yourself to think about what you want to change and how your life is becoming. Don't try not to think about the things that are wrong or bad, just think about the things you desire and how life will be when it's changed.

Don't think about being overweight or feeling fat. Focus your thoughts on your vision, how you will look and feel as you change.

To meditate is to ponder, imagine, think about and chew on mentally. While you drive, as you eat, or when you have a spare moment, meditate on your desires, visions and destiny.

Scriptures to meditate on:

Day 8
Ephesians 1:3-6 - Blessed be the God and Father of our Lord Jesus Christ, who has blessed us with every spiritual blessing in the heavenly places in Christ, just as <u>He chose us in Him before the foundation of the world</u>, that we should be holy and without blame before Him in love, <u>having predes-</u>

tined us to adoption as sons by Jesus Christ to Himself, according to the good pleasure of His will, to the praise of the glory of His grace, by which He has made us accepted in the Beloved.

Day 9
Ephesians 1:10-11 - . . .that in the dispensation of the fullness of the times He might gather together in one all things in Christ, both which are in heaven and which are on earth— in Him. In Him also we have obtained an inheritance, being predestined according to the purpose of Him who works all things according to the counsel of His will.

Day 10
Ephesians 2:10 - For we are His workmanship, created in Christ Jesus for good works, which God prepared beforehand that we should walk in them.

Day 11
Romans 8:29-32 - For whom He foreknew, He also predestined to be conformed to the image of His Son, that He might be the firstborn among many brethren. Moreover whom He predestined, these He also called; whom He called, these He also justified; and whom He justified, these He also glorified. What then shall we say to these things? If God is for us, who can be against us? He who did not spare His own Son, but delivered Him up for us all, how shall He not with Him also freely give us all things?

Day 12
Joshua 1:8 - This Book of the Law shall not depart

from your mouth, but you shall meditate in it day and night, that you may observe to do according to all that is written in it. For then you will make your way prosperous, and then you will have good success.

Day 13
I Timothy 4:15 - Meditate on these things; give yourself entirely to them, that your progress may be evident to all.

Day 14
Psalm 1:1-3 - Blessed is the man who walks not in the counsel of the ungodly, nor stands in the path of sinners, nor sits in the seat of the scornful; but his delight is in the law of the LORD, and in His law he meditates day and night. He shall be like a tree planted by the rivers of water, that brings forth its fruit in its season, whose leaf also shall not wither; and whatever he does shall prosper.

WEEK THREE

KNOWLEDGE - You must know the right things to accomplish the right things. Lack of knowledge will keep you from success.

The prophet Hosea tells us many of God's people are cut off from blessing because of a lack of knowledge. When we don't know the truths of God that bring success in life, we struggle and fail.

Most of us function off the knowledge we received as kids from parents, school, religion, and society. We must examine what we believe and think. If it is not in line with God's Word, it may be keeping us from God's will and God's best.

FAITH - Believe in yourself and believe in God to enable you to succeed.

Faith comes by hearing the Word of God (Romans 10:17). As we learn God's Word, faith will rise in our hearts. Confidence, trust, and faith in God are necessary to receive from God. Things don't just happen because God wants them to happen. We must walk by faith, not by sight (II Corinthians 5:7).

Jesus said over and over again, "Your faith has made you whole," and, "According to your faith be it unto you." If you will believe, God will go to work to bring change, renewal, healing, and blessings in your life.

Scriptures to meditate on:

Day 15
Hosea 4:6 - <u>My people are destroyed for lack of knowledge</u>. Because you have rejected knowledge, I also will reject you from being priest for Me; because you have forgotten the law of your God, I also will forget your children.

Day 16
Romans 12:2 - And do not be conformed to this world, <u>but be transformed by the renewing of your mind</u>, that you may prove what is that good and acceptable and <u>perfect will of God</u>.

Day 17
Ephesians 4:22-24 - . . . that you put off, concerning your former conduct, the old man which <u>grows corrupt</u> according to the deceitful lusts, and be renewed in the spirit of your mind, and that you <u>put on the new man</u> which was created according to God, in true righteousness and holiness.

Day 18
Colossians 3:1-2 - If then you were raised with Christ, <u>seek those things which are above</u>, where Christ is, sitting at the right hand of God. <u>Set your mind on things above, not on things on the earth</u>.

Day 19
Mark 11:22-24 - So Jesus answered and said to them, "<u>Have faith in God</u>. For assuredly, I say to you, whoever says to this mountain, 'Be removed and be cast into the sea,' and <u>does not doubt in his heart</u>, but believes that those things he says will come to pass, <u>he will have whatever he says</u>. Therefore I say to you, whatever things you ask when you pray, <u>believe that you receive them, and you will have them</u>."

Day 20
Matthew 8:5-10,13 Now when Jesus had entered Capernaum, a centurion came to Him, pleading with Him, saying, "Lord, my servant is lying at home paralyzed, dreadfully tormented." And Jesus said to him, "I will come and heal him." The centurion answered and said, "Lord, I am not worthy that You should come under my roof. <u>But only speak a word</u>, and my servant will be healed. For I also am a man

under authority, having soldiers under me. And I
say to this one, 'Go,' and he goes; and to another,
'Come,' and he comes; and to my servant, 'Do this,'
and he does it." When Jesus heard it, He marveled,
and said to those who followed, "Assuredly, I say
to you, I have not found such great faith, not even
in Israel! Then Jesus said to the centurion, "Go
your way; and <u>as you have believed, so let it be
done for you</u>." And his servant was healed that same
hour.

Day 21
Hebrews 11:1-3,6 - Now <u>faith is the substance of
things hoped for, the evidence of things not seen</u>.
For by it the elders obtained a good testimony. By
faith we understand that the worlds were framed
by the word of God, so that the things which are
seen were not made of things which are visible. But
<u>without faith it is impossible to please Him,</u> for he
who comes to God must believe that He is, and that
<u>He is a rewarder of those who diligently seek Him</u>.

Day 22
Proverbs 3:5-6 - <u>Trust in the LORD with all your
heart</u>, and lean not on your own understanding; in
all your ways <u>acknowledge Him</u>, and He shall direct your paths.

Day 23
Psalm 37:5-6 - <u>Commit your way to the LORD,</u>

<u>trust also in Him, and He shall bring it to pass</u>. He shall bring forth your righteousness as the light, and your justice as the noonday.

WEEK FOUR

RENEWING - Old thoughts and habits must be replaced with new thoughts and habits.

As we learn new scriptures and biblical truth, we must make sure we are renewing and not just gaining knowledge. Learning is part of the process of change, but we must release old, negative thoughts and focus on the new thoughts. Take off the old and put on the new.

Renewing the mind is exchanging old ways of thinking for new ways so that you think and believe like Jesus teaches us to. Those who never change will never move in God's will for their lives. The book of Proverbs teaches us that those who will not renew their minds are fools (Proverbs 9:7-9).

RELEASE - You must let go of things that will hold you down and keep you from changing.

There will be many thoughts, beliefs, and attitudes that we must release to move ahead in destiny. Letting go of the past, negative thoughts, and even negative people is a big part of change. Because many people will not release these things, they get stuck in mediocre lives and worldly ruts.

Examine those thoughts, attitudes, and people that may stop you from changing and moving ahead with the Lord.

REVIEW - "Re-view" every step you have taken.
We don't learn overnight. We learn by going over and over and over. Don't give up too quickly. Go over these things again and get these scriptures in your heart and life.

Scriptures to meditate on:

Day 24
Romans 8:5-6 - For those who live according to the flesh set their minds on the things of the flesh, but those who live according to the Spirit, the things of the Spirit. For to be carnally minded is death, but to be spiritually minded is life and peace.

Day 25
John 8:31-32 - Then Jesus said to those Jews who believed Him, "If you abide in My word, you are My disciples indeed. And you shall know the truth, and the truth shall make you free."

Day 26
Proverbs 4:20-23 - My son, give attention to my words; incline your ear to my sayings. Do not let them depart from your eyes; keep them in the midst of your heart; for they are life to those who find them, and health to all their flesh. Keep your heart with all diligence, for out of it spring the issues of life.

Day 27
James 1:22-25 - But be doers of the word, and not

hearers only, deceiving yourselves. For if anyone is a hearer of the word and not a doer, he is like a man observing his natural face in a mirror; for he observes himself, goes away, and immediately forgets what kind of man he was. But <u>he who looks into the perfect law of liberty</u> and continues in it, and is not a forgetful hearer but a <u>doer of the work, this one will be blessed in what he does</u>.

Day 28
Joshua 1:6-9 - <u>Be strong and of good courage</u>, for to this people you shall divide as an inheritance the land which I swore to their fathers to give them. Only <u>be strong and very courageous, that you may observe to do according to all the law</u> which Moses My servant commanded you; <u>do not turn from it to the right hand or to the left, that you may prosper wherever you go</u>. This Book of the Law shall not depart from your mouth, but you shall meditate in it day and night, that you may observe to do according to all that is written in it. <u>For then you will make your way prosperous, and then you will have good success</u>. Have I not commanded you? Be strong and of good courage; do not be afraid, nor be dismayed, for the LORD your God is with you wherever you go.

Day 29
Ephesians 6:10 - Finally, my brethren, <u>be strong in the Lord and in the power of His might</u>.

Day 30
Matthew 18:18-19 - Assuredly, I say to you, <u>what-</u>

ever you bind on earth will be bound in heaven, and whatever you loose on earth will be loosed in heaven. Again I say to you that if two of you agree on earth concerning anything that they ask, it will be done for them by My Father in heaven.

Day 31
I Corinthians 15:58 - Therefore, my beloved brethren, be steadfast, immovable, always abounding in the work of the Lord, knowing that your labor is not in vain in the Lord.

BIBLE
READING
PLAN

READ THE BIBLE
IN ONE YEAR:
A DAILY READING PLAN

Day 1	Genesis 1:1 - 3:8 Matthew 1:1 - 1:22	Day 13	Genesis 27:41 - 30:1 Matthew 9:30 - 10:13
Day 2	Genesis 3:9 - 5:22 Matthew 1:23 - 2:19	Day 14	Genesis 30:2 - 31:22 Matthew 10:14 - 10:35
Day 3	Genesis 5:23 - 8:8 Matthew 2:20 - 4:1	Day 15	Genesis 31:23 - 32:31 Matthew 10:36 - 11:15
Day 4	Genesis 8:9 - 10:21 Matthew 4:2 - 4:23	Day 16	Genesis 32:32 - 35:12 Matthew 11:16 - 12:7
Day 5	Genesis 10:22 - 13:1 Matthew 4:24 - 5:20	Day 17	Genesis 35:13 - 37:4 Matthew 12:8 - 12:29
Day 6	Genesis 13:2 - 16:2 Matthew 5:21 - 5:42	Day 18	Genesis 37:5 - 39:2 Matthew 12:30 - 13:1
Day 7	Genesis 16:3 - 18:23 Matthew 5:43 - 6:16	Day 19	Genesis 39:3 - 41:20 Matthew 13:2 - 13:23
Day 8	Genesis 18:24 - 20:16 Matthew 6:17 - 7:4	Day 20	Genesis 41:21 - 42:27 Matthew 13:24 - 13:45
Day 9	Genesis 20:17 - 23:4 Matthew 7:5 - 7:26	Day 21	Genesis 42:28 - 44:19 Matthew 13:46 - 14:9
Day 10	Genesis 23:5 - 24:48 Matthew 7:27 - 8:19	Day 22	Genesis 44:20 - 46:21 Matthew 14:10 - 14:31
Day 11	Genesis 24:49 - 26:11 Matthew 8:20 - 9:7	Day 23	Genesis 46:22 - 48:20 Matthew 14:32 - 15:17
Day 12	Genesis 26:12 - 27:40 Matthew 9:8 - 9:29	Day 24	Genesis 48:21 - 50:26 Exodus 1:1 - 1:3 Matthew 15:18 - 15:39

Day 25	Exodus 1:4 - 3:20 Matthew 16:1 - 16:22	Day 37	Exodus 28:11 - 29:31 Matthew 23:19 - 24:1
Day 26	Exodus 3:21 - 6:8 Matthew 16:23 - 17:16	Day 38	Exodus 29:32 - 31:11 Matthew 24:2 - 24:23
Day 27	Exodus 6:9 - 8:17 Matthew 17:17 - 18:11	Day 39	Exodus 31:12 - 33:22 Matthew 24:24 - 24:45
Day 28	Exodus 8:18 - 10:14 Matthew 18:12 - 18:33	Day 40	Exodus 33:23 - 35:28 Matthew 24:46 - 25:16
Day 29	Exodus 10:15 - 12:39 Matthew 18:34 - 19:20	Day 41	Exodus 35:29 - 37:19 Matthew 25:17 - 25:38
Day 30	Exodus 12:40 - 14:30 Matthew 19:21 - 20:12	Day 42	Exodus 37:20 - 39:23 Matthew 25:39 - 26:14
Day 31	Exodus 14:31 - 16:36 Matthew 20:13 - 20:34	Day 43	Exodus 39:24 - 40:38 Leviticus 1:1 - 1:6 Matthew 26:15 - 26:36
Day 32	Exodus 17:1 - 19:21 Matthew 21:1 - 21:22	Day 44	Leviticus 1:7 - 4:20 Matthew 26:37 - 26:58
Day 33	Exodus 19:22 - 21:34 Matthew 21:23 - 21:44	Day 45	Leviticus 4:21 - 6:30 Matthew 26:59 - 27:5
Day 34	Exodus 21:35 - 23:31 Matthew 21:45 - 22:20	Day 46	Leviticus 7:1 - 8:26 Matthew 27:6 - 27:27
Day 35	Exodus 23:32 - 26:4 Matthew 22:21 - 22:42	Day 47	Leviticus 8:27 - 11:10 Matthew 27:28 - 27:49
Day 36	Exodus 26:5 - 28:10 Matthew 22:43 - 23:18	Day 48	Leviticus 11:11 - 13:19 Matthew 27:50 - 28:5

285

293

294

Day 347 Daniel 7:15 - 9:22
Revelation 1:5 - 2:5

Day 348 Daniel 9:23 - 11:37
Revelation 2:6 - 2:26

Day 349 Daniel 11:38 - 12:13
Hosea 1:1 - 4:3
Revelation 2:27 -
3:18

Day 350 Hosea 4:4 - 8:5
Revelation 3:19 - 5:6

Day 351 Hosea 8:6 - 12:10
Revelation 5:7 - 6:13

Day 352 Hosea 12:11 - 14:9
Joel 1:1 - 2:14
Revelation 6:14 -
7:17

Day 353 Joel 2:15 - 3:21
Amos 1:1 - 2:9
Revelation 8:1 - 9:8

Day 354 Amos 2:10 - 6:1
Revelation 9:9 - 10:8

Day 355 Amos 6:2 - 9:15
Obadiah 1:1 - 1:4
Revelation 10:9 -
11:18

Day 356 Obadiah 1:5 - 1:21
Jonah 1:1 - 4:9
Revelation 11:19 -
13:3

Day 357 Jonah 4:10 - 4:11
Micah 1:1 - 5:7
Revelation 13:4 -
14:6

Day 358 Micah 5:8 - 7:20
Nahum 1:1 - 2:4
Revelation 14:7 -
15:7

Day 359 Nahum 2:5 - 3:19
Habakkuk 1:1 - 2:18
Revelation 15:8 -
16:20

Day 360 Habakkuk 2:19 -
3:19
Zephaniah 1:1 - 3:9
Revelation 16:21 -
18:2

Day 361 Zephaniah 3:10 -
3:20
Haggai 1:1 - 2:23
Zechariah 1:1 - 1:14
Revelation 18:3 -
18:23

Day 362 Zechariah 1:15 - 6:8
Revelation 18:24 -
19:20

Day 363 Zechariah 6:9 - 10:2
Revelation 19:21 -
21:5

Day 364 Zechariah 10:3 -
14:13
Revelation 21:6 -
21:26

Day 365 Zechariah 14:14 -
14:21
Malachi 1:1 - 4:7
Revelation 21:27 -
22:21

BOOKS BY
CASEY AND WENDY
TREAT

Battle of the Sexes
Wendy Treat

Being Spiritually Minded
Casey Treat

The Benefits of Godly Wisdom
Casey Treat

Blueprint For Life
Casey Treat

Building Leaders That Build A Church
Casey Treat

Errors of the Prosperity Gospel
Casey Treat

Fighting for Excellence in Leadership
Casey Treat

Fulfilling Your God-Given Destiny
Casey Treat

Leading People in Church Growth
Casey Treat

Living the New Life
Casey Treat

Positive Childbirth
Casey and Wendy Treat

Renewing the Mind
Casey Treat

Woman! Get in Your Place
Wendy Treat

Won By One
Wendy Treat

Books can be ordered from
Solomon's Books and Gifts
PO Box 98800
Seattle, WA 98198
(206) 870-3670